THE KNEELING CHRISTIAN

This is more than a feel-good book. This is a book that requires action on the part of the reader. Most importantly, however: let the Holy Spirit lead you in your prayers. May the Lord's will be done.

– The Publisher

THE KNEELING CHRISTIAN

If ye have faith and doubt not
... all things, whatsoever ye shall ask in
prayer, believing, ye shall receive.

ALBERT RICHARDSON

Cover Design: BookCoverLabs.com

Editors: Sheila Wilkinson and Ruth Zetek

Printed in the United States of America

Aneko Press – *Our Readers Matter*™

www.anekopress.com

Aneko Press, Life Sentence Publishing, and our logos are trademarks of

Life Sentence Publishing, Inc.
203 E. Birch Street
P.O. Box 652
Abbotsford, WI 54405

RELIGION / Christian Life / Prayer

Paperback ISBN: 978-1-62245-329-0

eBook ISBN: 978-1-62245-330-6

10 9 8 7 6 5 4 3 2 1

Available where books are sold

Share this book on Facebook:

CONTENTS

CHAPTER 1

GOD'S GREAT DESIRE

God wondered." This is a striking thought. The very boldness of the idea ought to arrest the attention of every earnest Christian man, woman, and child. A wondering God. How staggered we might be if we knew the cause of God's "wonder." Yet we apparently find it to be a very little thing. But if we are willing to consider the matter carefully, we shall discover it to be of greatest possible importance to every believer on the Lord Jesus Christ. Nothing else is so momentous – so vital – to our spiritual welfare.

God *wondered that there was no intercessor* (Isa. 59:16). But this was in the days of long ago, before the coming of the Lord Jesus Christ, *full of grace and truth*. This was before the outpouring of the Holy Spirit, full of grace and power, who *helps our weakness; … but the Spirit itself makes entreaty for us* (Rom. 8:26). Yes, this was before the truly amazing promises of our Savior regarding prayer, before men knew very much about prayer in the days when sacrifices for their sins loomed larger in their eyes than supplication for other sinners.

Oh, how great must God's wonder be today. For how few

there are among us who know what prevailing prayer really is. Every one of us would confess that we believe in prayer, yet how many of us truly believe in the power of prayer? Now, before we go a step further, may I most earnestly implore you not to hurry as you read what is contained in these chapters. Much, very much, depends upon the way in which every reader receives what is recorded here. For everything depends upon prayer.

Why are many Christians so often defeated? Because they pray so little. Why are many church workers so often discouraged and disheartened? Because they pray so little.

The secret of all failure is our failure in secret prayer.

Why do most Christian leaders see so few brought *out of darkness to light* by their ministry? Because they pray so little. Why are our churches simply not on fire for God? Because there is so little real prayer.

The Lord Jesus is as powerful today as ever before. The Lord Jesus is as anxious for men to be saved as ever before. His arm is not shortened that it cannot save, but He cannot stretch forth His arm unless we pray more – and more genuinely.

We may be assured of this: The secret of all failure is our failure in secret prayer.

If God *wondered* in the days of Isaiah, we need not be surprised to find that in the days of His flesh, our Lord *marveled*. He marveled at the unbelief of some, unbelief which actually prevented Him from doing any mighty work in their cities (Mark 6:6).

But we must remember that those who were guilty of this unbelief saw no beauty in Him that they should desire Him or believe on Him. What then must He marvel at today, when He sees among us who truly love and adore Him, so few who really wake themselves up to take hold of Him (Isa. 64:7)? Surely, nothing is so absolutely astonishing as a practically prayerless Christian. These are eventful and ominous days. In fact, there are many evidences that these are *the last days* in which God promised to pour out His Spirit, the Spirit of supplication, upon all flesh (Joel 2:28). Yet the vast majority of professing Christians scarcely know what *supplication* means, and many of our churches not only have no prayer meetings, but sometimes unblushingly condemn such meetings and even ridicule them.

The Church of England, recognizing the importance of worship and prayer, expects her clergy to read prayers in church every morning and evening.

But when this is done, is it not often in an empty church? And are not the prayers frequently raced through at a pace which hinders real worship? "Common prayer" too is often rather vague and indefinite. And what of those churches where the old-fashioned weekly prayer meeting is retained? Would not *weakly* be the more appropriate word? C. H. Spurgeon had the joy of being able to say that he conducted a prayer meeting every Monday night, "which scarcely ever numbers less than from a thousand to twelve hundred attendants."

My brothers, have we ceased to believe in prayer? If you still hold your weekly gathering for prayer, is it not a fact that the great majority of your church members never come near it? Yes, and never even think of coming near it. Why is this? Whose fault is it?

"Only a prayer meeting" – how often we have heard the utterance. How many of those reading these words really enjoy a prayer meeting? Is it a joy or just a duty? Please forgive me for asking so many questions and for pointing out what appears to be a perilous weakness and a lamentable shortcoming in our churches. We are not out to criticize, much less to condemn. Anybody can do that. Our yearning desire is to stir up Christians *to take hold of* God as never before. We wish to encourage, to hearten, to uplift.

We are never so high as when we are on our knees.

We are never so high as when we are on our knees.

Criticize? Who dares criticize another? When we look back upon the past and remember how much prayerlessness there has been in one's own life, words of criticism of others wither away on the lips.

But we believe the time has come when the individual and the church need a clarion call to prayer.

Now, dare we face this question of prayer? It seems a foolish query, for is not prayer a part and parcel of all religions? Yet we venture to ask our readers to look at this matter fairly and squarely. Do I really believe that prayer is a power? Is prayer the greatest power on earth, or is it not? Does prayer indeed "move the Hand that moves the world"?

Do God's prayer commands really concern me? Do the promises of God concerning prayer still hold true? We have all been muttering, "Yes, Yes, Yes," as we read these questions. We dare not say "No" to any one of them. And yet, has it ever occurred to you that our Lord never gave an unnecessary or an optional command? Do we really believe that our Lord never made a promise which He could not, or would not, fulfill? Our Savior's three great commands for definite action were:

Pray ye
 Do ye
  Go ye

Are we obeying Him? How often His command *Do this* is reiterated by our preachers today. One might almost think it was His only command. How seldom we are reminded of His bidding to pray and to go. Yet, without obedience to the *Pray ye*, it is of little or no use at all either to *Do this* or to *Go*.

In fact, it can be shown that all desire of success and all failure in the spiritual life and in Christian work is due to defective or insufficient prayer. Unless we pray aright, we cannot live aright or serve aright. This may appear, at first sight, to be gross exaggeration, but the more we think it over in the light Scripture throws upon it, the more convinced we will be of the truth of this statement.

Now, as we begin once more to see what the Bible has to say about this mysterious and wonderful subject, shall we endeavor to read some of our Lord's promises, as though we had never heard them before. What will the effect be?

Some twenty years ago, I was studying in a theological college. Early one morning, a fellow student, who is today one of England's foremost missionaries, burst into the room holding an open Bible in his hands. Although he was preparing for Holy Orders, he was at that time only a young convert to Christ.

He had gone up to the university caring for none of these things. Popular, clever, and athletic, he had already won a place among the smart set of his college, when Christ claimed him. He accepted the Lord Jesus as his personal Savior and became a keen follower of his Master. The Bible was, comparatively, a new book to him, and as a result, he was constantly making "discoveries." On that memorable day on which he invaded my quietude with his face all aglow with mingled joy and surprise, he cried, "Do you believe this? Is it really true?"

"Believe what?" I asked, glancing at the open Bible with some astonishment.

"Why, this," and he read in eager tones Matthew 21:21-22: "*If ye have faith and doubt not, … all things, whatsoever ye shall ask in prayer, believing, ye shall receive.* Do you believe it? Is it true?"

"Yes," I replied with much surprise at his excitement, "of course, it's true; of course, I believe it." Yet, through my mind there flashed all manner of thoughts.

"Well, that's a very wonderful promise," said he. "It seems to me to be absolutely limitless. Why don't we pray more?" And he went away, leaving me thinking hard. I had never looked at those verses quite in that way.

As the door closed upon that eager young follower of the Master, I had a vision of my Savior and His love and His power such as I never had before. I had a vision of a life of prayer, yes, and limitless power, which I saw depended upon two things – faith and prayer. For the moment, I was thrilled. I fell on my knees, and as I bowed before my Lord, what thoughts surged through my mind, what hopes and aspirations flooded my soul. God was speaking to me in an extraordinary way. This was a great call to prayer. But to my shame let it be said, I heeded not that call.

Where did I fail? True, I prayed a little more than before, but nothing much seemed to happen. Why? Was it because

I did not see what a high standard the Savior requires in the inner life of those who would pray successfully?

Was it because my life had failed to measure up to the "perfect love" standard so beautifully described in the thirteenth chapter of 1 Corinthians? For, after all, prayer is not just putting into action good resolutions to pray. Like David, we need to cry, *Create in me a clean heart, O God*, before we can pray aright (Psalm 51:10). And the inspired words of the apostle of love need to be heeded today as much as ever before: *Beloved, if our heart does not condemn us, then we have confidence in God; and whatsoever we ask, we receive of him* (1 John 3:21-22).

...prayer is not just putting into action good resolutions to pray.

"True and I believe it." Yes, indeed, it is a limitless promise, and yet how little we realize it, how little we claim from Christ. And our Lord marvels at our unbelief. But if we could only read the Gospels for the first time, what an amazing book it would seem. Should we not *marvel* and *wonder*? And today I pass on that great call to you. Will you give heed to it? Will you profit by it? Or shall it fall on deaf ears and leave you prayerless?

Fellow Christians, let us wake up. The Devil is blinding our eyes. He is endeavoring to prevent us from facing this question of prayer. These pages are written by special request. But many months have passed since that request came.

Every attempt to write has been frustrated, and even now I am conscious of a strange reluctance to do so. Some mysterious power seems to be restraining my hand. Do we realize that there is nothing the Devil dreads so much as prayer? His great concern is to keep us from praying. He loves to see us "up to our eyes" in work, provided we do not pray. He does not fear that we are eager and earnest Bible students, provided we are little in prayer. Someone has wisely said, "Satan laughs at our toiling, mocks at our wisdom, but trembles when we pray." All this is so familiar to us, but do we really pray? If not, then failure will dog our footsteps, whatever signs of apparent success there may be.

Let us never forget that the greatest thing we can do for God or for man is to pray. For we can accomplish far more by our prayers than by our work. Prayer is omnipotent; it can do anything that God can do. When we pray, God works. All fruitfulness in service is the outcome of the workers' prayers or of those who are holding up holy hands on their behalf. We all know how to pray, but perhaps many of us need to cry as the disciples did of old, *Lord, teach us to pray.*

> *O Thou by Whom we come to God –*
> *The Life, the Truth, the Way,*
> *The path of prayer Thyself hast trod;*
> *Lord, teach us now to pray.*

CHAPTER 2

ALMOST INCREDIBLE PROMISES

W hen we stand with Christ in glory, looking o'er life's finished story," the most amazing feature of that life as it is looked back upon will be its prayerlessness.

We shall be beside ourselves with astonishment that we spent so little time in real intercession. It will be our turn to *wonder*.

In our Lord's last discourse to His loved ones, just before the most wonderful of all prayers, the Master again and again held out His kingly golden scepter and said, as it were, "What is your request? It shall be granted unto you, even unto the whole of My kingdom."

Do we believe this? We must, if we believe our Bibles. Shall we just read over very quietly and thoughtfully one of our Lord's promises, reiterated so many times? If we had never read them before, we should open our eyes in bewilderment, for these promises are almost incredible. From the lips of any mere man, they would be quite unbelievable. But it is the Lord of heaven and earth Who speaks, and He is speaking at the most solemn moment of His life.

It is the eve of His death and passion. It is a farewell message. Now listen.

Verily, verily, I say unto you, He that believes in me, the works that I do he shall do also; and greater works than these shall he do because I go unto my Father. And whatsoever ye shall ask the Father in my name, that will I do, that the Father may be glorified in the Son. If ye ask any thing in my name, I will do it (John 14:12-14). Now, could any words be plainer or clearer than these? Could any promise be greater or grander? Has anyone else, anywhere, at any time, ever offered so much?

If ye abide in me and my words abide in you, ye shall ask what ye will, and it shall be done unto you.

How staggered those disciples must have been. Surely they could scarcely believe their own ears. But that promise is made also to you and to me.

And, lest there should be any mistake on their part, or on ours, our Lord repeats Himself a few moments afterwards. Yes, and the Holy Spirit bids John record those words again. *If ye abide in me and my words abide in you, ye shall ask what ye will, and it shall be done unto you. In this is my Father [glorified], in that ye bear much fruit; and in this manner ye shall be my disciples* (John 15:7-8).

These words are of such grave importance, and so momentous, that the Savior of the world is not content even with a threefold utterance of them. He urges His disciples to obey His command *to ask*. In fact, He tells them that one sign of their being His friends will be the obedience to His commands in all things (John 15:14). Then He once more repeats His wishes: *Ye have not chosen me, but I have chosen you and ordained you, that ye should go and bring forth fruit, and that your fruit should remain; that whatever ye shall ask of the Father in my name, he may give it unto you* (John 15:16).

One would think that our Lord had now made it plain enough that He wanted them to pray, that He demanded their prayers, and that without prayer they could accomplish nothing. But to our intense surprise, He returns again to the same subject, saying very much the same words.

And in that day ye shall ask me nothing [ask Me no question (Revised Standard Version margin note)]. *Verily, verily, I say unto you, Whatever ye shall ask the Father in my name, he will give you. Until now ye have asked nothing in my name; ask, and ye shall receive, that your joy may be fulfilled* (John 16:23-24).

Never before had our Lord laid such stress on any promise or command – never. This truly marvelous promise is given six times over. Six times, almost in the same breath, our Savior commands us to ask whatsoever we will. This is the greatest, the most wonderful promise ever made to man. Yet most people, Christian people, practically ignore it. Is it not so?

The exceeding greatness of the promise seems to overwhelm us. Yet we know that He *is able to do exceeding abundantly above all that we ask or think* (Eph. 3:20). So our blessed Master gives the final exhortation, before He is seized and bound and scourged, before His gracious lips are silenced on the cross: *ye shall ask in my name, ... for the Father himself loves you* (John 16:26-27). We have often spent much time in reflecting upon our Lord's seven words from the cross. And it is well we should do so. Have we ever spent one hour in meditating upon this, our Savior's sevenfold invitation to pray?

Today He sits on the throne of His majesty on high, and He holds out to us the scepter of His power. Shall we touch it and tell Him our desires? He bids us take of His treasures. He yearns to grant us *according to the riches of His glory*, that we may *be strengthened with might by his Spirit in the inner man*. He tells us that our strength and our fruitfulness depend upon our prayers. He reminds us that our very joy depends upon answered prayer (Eph. 3:16).

And yet we allow the Devil to persuade us to neglect prayer. He makes us believe that we can do more by our own efforts than by our prayers, by our conversations with men than by our intercession with God. It escapes one's comprehension that so little heed should be given to our Lord's sevenfold invitation – command – promise. How dare we work for Christ without being much on our knees? Quite recently an earnest Christian worker, a Sunday school teacher and church member, wrote me, saying, "I have never had an answer to prayer in all my life." But why? Is God a liar? Is God not trustworthy? Do His promises count for nothing? Doesn't He mean what He says? Doubtless, there are many reading these words who in their hearts are saying the same thing as that Christian worker. Edward Payson is right when he says, "If we would do much for God, we must ask much of God.... Pray, then, my dear brother, pray, pray, pray." If our prayers are not answered, or always answered but not necessarily granted, the fault must be entirely in ourselves and not in God. God delights to answer prayer, and He has given us His word that He will answer.

Fellow laborers in His vineyard, it is quite evident that

our Master desires us to ask and to ask much. He tells us we glorify Him by doing so. Nothing is beyond the scope of prayer, which is not beyond the will of God, and we do not desire to go beyond His will.

We dare not say that our Lord's words are not true. Yet somehow or other, few Christians really seem to believe them. What holds us back? What seals our lips? What keeps us from making much of prayer? Do we doubt His love? Never. He gave His life for us and to us. Do we doubt the Father's love? No. *The Father Himself loves you*, said Christ when urging His disciples to pray.

Do we doubt His power? Not for a moment. Has He not said, *All power is given unto me in heaven and in earth. Go ye ... and, behold, I am with you always* (Matt. 28:18-20)? Do we doubt His wisdom? Do we mistrust His choice for us? Not for a moment. And yet, very few of His followers consider prayer worthwhile. Of course, they would deny this, but actions speak louder than words. Are we afraid to put God to the test? He has said we may do so. *Bring ye all the tithes into the storehouse, ... and prove me now in this, said the LORD of the hosts, if I will not open you the windows of heaven and pour you out a blessing that there shall not be room enough to receive it* (Mal. 3:10). Whenever God makes us a promise, let us boldly say, as did the apostle Paul, *I believe God, that it shall be even as it was told me* (Acts 27:25).

Shall we begin today to be people of prayer, even if we have never been so before? Let us not put it off until a more convenient time. God wants me to pray. The dear Savior wants me to pray. So much, in fact everything, depends upon prayer. How dare we hold back? Let every one of us ask on our knees this question: "If no one on earth prayed for the salvation of sinners more fervently or more frequently than I do, how many of them would be converted to God through prayer?"

Do we spend ten minutes a day in prayer? Do we consider it important enough for that? Ten minutes a day on our knees in prayer when the kingdom of heaven can be had for the asking. Ten minutes? It seems a very inadequate portion of our time to spend in taking hold of God (Isa. 64:7).

And is it prayer when we "say" our prayers, or are we just repeating daily a few phrases, which have become practically meaningless, while our thoughts are wandering hither and thither?

If God were to answer the words we repeated on our knees this morning, would we know it? Would we recognize the answer? Do we even remember what we asked for? He does answer. He has given us His word for it. He always answers every real prayer of faith, but we shall see what the Bible has to say on this point in a later chapter. We are now thinking of the amount of time we spend in prayer.

"How often do you pray?" was the question put to a Christian woman. "Three times a day, and all the day beside," was the quick reply. But how many are like that? Is prayer to me just a duty, or is it a privilege – a pleasure, a real joy, a necessity?

Let us take a fresh look at Christ in all His glory and a fresh glimpse of all the *riches of His glory*, which He places at our disposal, and of all the mighty power given unto Him. Then let us take a fresh look at the world and all its needs. (And the world was never as needy as it is today.)

The wonder is not that we pray so little, but that we can

ever get up from our knees if we realize our own need, the needs of our home and our loved ones, the needs of our pastor and the church, the needs of our city in our country of the heathen and Islamic world. All these needs can be met by the riches of God in Christ Jesus.

The apostle Paul had no doubt about this nor have we. Yes, *my God shall supply all your need according to his riches in glory by Christ Jesus* (Phil. 4:19). But to share His riches, we must pray, *for the same Lord over all is rich unto all that call upon him* (Rom. 10:12).

...only the Holy Spirit can wake us up to take hold of God.

The importance of prayer is so great that God has taken care to anticipate all the excuses or objections we may be likely to make. Men plead their weakness or infirmity, or they declare they do not know how to pray.

God foresaw this inability ages ago. Did He not inspire Paul to say, *And likewise also the Spirit helps our weakness, for we know not how to pray as we ought, but the Spirit itself makes entreaty for us with groanings which cannot be uttered. But he that searches the hearts knows what is the desire of the Spirit, that according to the will of God, he makes entreaty for the saints* (Rom. 8:26-27).

Yes. Every provision is made for us. But only the Holy Spirit can *wake us up to take hold of* God. And if we yield ourselves to the Spirit's promptings, we shall most assuredly follow the example of the apostles of old, who gave themselves to prayer and *continued with one accord in prayer and supplication* (Acts 1:14).

We may rest assured of this: A man's influence in the world can be gauged not by his eloquence, or his zeal, or his orthodoxy, or his energy, but by his prayers. Yes, and we will go further and maintain that no man can live aright who does not pray aright.

We may work for Christ from morning till night; we may spend much time in Bible study; we may be earnest and faithful and acceptable in our preaching and in our individual dealing, but none of these things can be truly effective unless we are much in prayer. We shall only be full of good works but not *fruitful in every good work* (Col. 1:10). To be little with God in prayer is to be little for God in service. Much secret prayer means much public power. Yet is it not a fact that while our organizing is almost perfect, our agonizing in prayer is almost lost?

We are wondering why the revival delays its coming. Only one thing can delay it, and that is lack of prayer. All revivals have been the outcome of prayer. One sometimes longs for the voice of an archangel, but what good would that be if the voice of Christ Himself does not stir us up to pray? It seems almost impertinent for anyone to take up the cry when our Savior has put forth His "limitless" promises. Yet we feel that something should be done, and we believe that the Holy Spirit is prompting His people to remind themselves and others of Christ's words and power. No words of mine can impress others with the value of prayer, the need of prayer, and the omnipotence of prayer.

But these utterances go forth steeped in prayer that God the Holy Spirit will Himself convict Christian men and women of the sin of prayerlessness and drive them to their knees to call upon God day and night in burning, believing, prevailing intercession. The Lord Jesus, now in the heavenlies, beckons to us to fall upon our knees and claim the riches of His grace.

No one dares prescribe for another how long a time they ought to spend in prayer, nor do we suggest that people should make a vow to pray so many minutes or hours a day. Of course, the Bible command is to *pray without ceasing.* This is evidently the "attitude of prayer" that becomes the attitude of one's life.

Here we are speaking of definite acts of prayer. Have you ever timed your prayers? We believe that most of our readers would be amazed and confounded if they did time themselves.

Some years ago, I faced this prayer question. I felt that for me at least one hour a day was the minimum time that I should spend in prayer. I carefully noted a record of my prayer life every day. As time passed, I met a working man who was being very used by God. When asked to what he chiefly attributed his success, this man quietly replied, "Well, I could not get on without two hours a day of private prayer."

Then a Spirit-filled missionary from overseas crossed my path. He told very humbly of the wonderful things God was doing through his ministry. (One could see all along that God was given all the praise and all the glory.) "I find it necessary, oftentimes, to spend four hours a day in prayer," said this missionary.

And we remember how the greatest missionary of all sometimes spent whole nights in prayer. Why? Our blessed Lord did not pray simply as an example to us; He never did things merely as an example. He prayed because He needed to pray. As perfect Man, prayer was a necessity to Him. How much more is it necessary to you and me?

"Four hours a day in prayer!" exclaimed a man who is

giving his whole life to Christian work as a medical missionary. "Four hours? Give me ten minutes and I'm done." That was an honest and a brave confession, even if a sad one. Yet, if some of us were to speak out as honestly, what would we say?

Now, it was not by accident that these men crossed my path. God was speaking through them. It was just another "call to prayer" from the *God of patience*, who is also a "God of comfort" (Rom. 15:5). When their quiet message had sunk into my soul, a book came into my hands, "by chance," as people say. It told briefly and simply the story of

Do we really desire to do God's will?

John Hyde, "Praying Hyde," as he came to be called. Just as God sent John the Baptist to prepare the way of our Lord at His first coming, so He sent in these last days John the Prayer to make straight paths for His coming again. "Praying Hyde" – what a name. As I read of this marvelous life of prayer, I began to ask, "Have I ever prayed?"

I found others were asking the same question. One lady, who is noted for her wonderful intercession, wrote me, saying, "When I laid down this book, I began to think I had never in all my life really prayed."

But here we must leave the matter. Shall we get on our knees before God and allow His Holy Spirit to search us through and through? Are we sincere? Do we really desire to do God's will? Do we really believe His promises? If so, will it not lead us to spend more time on our knees before God? Do not vow to pray "so much" a day. Resolve to pray much; but prayer, to be precious, must be spontaneous and not from constraint.

But we must bear in mind that mere resolutions to

take more time for prayer and conquer reluctance to pray will not prove effective unless there is a wholehearted and absolute surrender to the Lord Jesus Christ. If we have never taken this step, we must take it now if we desire to be people of prayer.

I am quite certain of this fact: God wants me to pray; He wants you to pray. The question is: Are we willing to pray?

Gracious Savior, pour out upon us the fullness of the Holy Spirit that we may indeed become *kneeling Christians.*

> *To God your every want*
>   *In instant prayer display.*
> *Pray always; pray and never faint:*
>   *Pray! Without ceasing, pray.*

CHAPTER 3

ASK OF ME AND I WILL GIVE

God wants me to pray, to be much in prayer, because all success in spiritual work is dependent on prayer.

A preacher who prays little may see some results of his labors, but if he does, it will be because someone, somewhere, is praying for him. The "fruit" is the prayer's – not the preacher's. How surprised some of us preachers will be one day, when the Lord shall *reward everyone according to their works.*

"Lord, those were my converts. It was I who conducted that mission at which so many were brought into the fold." Ah, yes, I did the preaching, the pleading, the persuading; but was it "I" who did the praying? Every convert is the result of the Holy Spirit's pleading in answer to the prayers of some believer.

O God, grant that such surprise may not be ours. O Lord, teach us to pray.

We have had a vision of God pleading for prayer from His children. How am I treating that call? Can I say, with the apostle Paul, *I was not disobedient unto the heavenly vision*? Again, we repeat, if there are any regrets in heaven, the greatest will be that we spent so little time in real intercession while we were on earth.

Think of the wide sweep of prayer. *Ask of me, and I shall give thee the Gentiles for thine inheritance and unto the uttermost parts of the earth for thy possession* (Psalm 2:8). Yet many people do not trouble to bring even the little details of their own lives to God in prayer, and nine out of ten Christian people never think of praying for the heathen.

One is staggered at the unwillingness of Christians to pray. Perhaps it is because they have never experienced, or even heard of, convincing answers to prayer.

In this chapter we are setting out to do the impossible. What is that? We long to bring home to the heart and conscience of every reader the power of prayer. We venture to describe this as impossible. For if men will not believe and act upon our Lord's promises and commands, how can we expect them to be persuaded by any mere human exhortations?

But do you remember that our Lord, when speaking to His disciples, asked them to believe that He was in the Father and the Father in Him? Then he added: If you cannot believe My bare word about this, *believe Me for the very works' sake* (John 14:11). It was as if He said, "If My Person, My sanctified life, and My wonderful words do not elicit belief in Me, then look at My works: Surely they are sufficient to compel belief. Believe Me because of what I do."

Then He went on to promise that if they would believe, they would do greater works than these. It was after this utterance that He gave the first of those six wonderful promises about prayer. The inference surely is that those *greater works* are to be done only as the outcome of prayer.

May the disciple, therefore, follow the Master's method? Fellow worker, if you fail to grasp, fail to trust our Lord's astounding promises regarding prayer, will you not believe them *for the very works' sake*? That is, will you not believe because of those *greater works*, which men and women are performing today, or the works which the Lord Jesus is doing through their prayerful cooperation?

God can do more through our prayers than through our preaching.

What are we "out for"? What is our real aim in life? Surely, we desire most of all to be abundantly fruitful in the Master's service. We seek not position, or prominence, or power. But we do long to be fruitful servants. Then we must be much in prayer. God can do more through our prayers than through our preaching.

A. J. Gordon once said, "You can do more than pray, after you have prayed; but you can never do more than pray, until you have prayed." If only we would believe this.

A lady in India was cast down through the failure of her life and work. She was a devoted missionary, but somehow conversions never resulted from her ministry. The Holy Spirit seemed to say to her, "Pray more." But she resisted the promptings of the Spirit for some time.

"At length," said she, "I set apart much of my time for prayer. I did it in fear and trembling lest my fellow workers should complain that I was shirking my work. After a few weeks, I began to see men and women accepting Christ as their Savior. Moreover, the whole district was soon awakened, and the work of all the other missionaries was blessed as never before. God did more in six months than I had succeeded in doing in six years. And," she added, "no one ever accused me of shirking my duty."

Another lady missionary in India felt the same call to pray. She gave much time to prayer. No opposition came from without, but it did come from within. But she persisted, and in two years the baptized converts increased sixfold.

God promised that He would *pour upon the house of David ... the Spirit of grace and of prayer* (Zech. 12:10). He also told Joel that He would *pour out my Spirit upon all flesh* (Joel 2:28). How much of that Spirit of supplication is ours? Surely, we must get that Spirit at all costs? Yet if we are not willing to spend time in supplication, God must withhold His Spirit, and we become numbered among those who are *resisting the Spirit* and possibly *quenching* the Spirit. Has not our Lord promised the Holy Spirit to them that ask (Luke 11:13)? Are not the very converts from heathendom putting some of us to shame?

A few years ago, when in India, I had the great joy of seeing something of Pandita Ramabai's work. She had a boarding school of fifteen hundred Hindu girls. One day some of these girls came with their Bibles and asked a lady missionary what Luke 12:49 meant: *I am come to cast fire into the earth; and what do I desire, except that it be kindled?* The missionary tried to put them off with an evasive answer, not being sure herself what those words meant. But they were not satisfied, so they determined to pray for this fire. And as they prayed and because they prayed, the very fire of heaven came into their souls. A very Pentecost from above was granted them. No wonder they continued to pray.

A party of these girls upon whom God had poured the

"Spirit of supplication" came to a mission house where I spent some weeks. "May we stay here in your town and pray for your work?" they asked.

The missionary did not entertain the idea with any great enthusiasm. He felt that they ought to be at school and not "gadding about" the country. But they only asked for a hall or barn where they could pray, and we all value prayers on our behalf. So their request was granted, and the good man sat down to his evening meal, thinking. As the evening wore on, a native pastor came around. He broke down completely. He explained, with tears running down his face, that God's Holy Spirit had convicted him of sin and that he felt compelled to come and openly confess his wrongdoing. He was quickly followed by one Christian after another, all under deep conviction of sin.

There was a remarkable time of blessing. Backsliders were restored, believers were sanctified, and heathen were brought into the fold, all because a few mere children were praying.

God is no respecter of persons. If anyone is willing to conform to His conditions, He will assuredly fulfill His promises. Does not our heart burn within us as we hear of God's wonderful power? And that power is ours for the asking. I know there are "conditions." But you and I can fulfill them all through Christ. And for those of us who cannot have the privilege of serving God in India or any other overseas mission, we may yet take our part in bringing down a like blessing. When the revival in Wales was at its height, a Welsh missionary wrote home, begging the people to pray that India might be moved in like manner. So the coal miners met daily at the pit entrance half an hour before dawn to pray for their comrade overseas. In a few weeks' time, the welcome message was sent home: "The blessing has come."

Isn't it splendid to know that by our prayers we can bring showers of blessing upon India, or Africa, or China, just as readily as we can get the few drops needed for our own little plot?

Many of us will recall the wonderful things that God did for Korea a few years ago, entirely in answer to prayer. A few missionaries decided to meet together to pray daily at noon. At the end of the month, one brother proposed that "as nothing had happened," the prayer meeting should be discontinued. "Let us each pray at home as we find it convenient," said he. The others, however, protested that they ought to spend even more time in prayer each day. So they continued the daily prayer meeting for four months. Then suddenly the blessing began to be poured out. Church services here and there were interrupted with weeping and confessing of sins. At length a mighty revival broke out. At one place during a Sunday evening service, the leading man in the church stood up and confessed that he had stolen 100 dollars in administering a widow's legacy. Immediately, conviction of sin swept the audience. That service did not end until two o'clock on Monday morning. God's wondrous power was felt as never before. And when the church was purified, many sinners found salvation.

Multitudes flocked to the churches out of curiosity. Some came to mock, but fear laid hold of them, and they stayed to pray. Among the curious was a brigand chief, the leader of a robber band. He was convicted and converted. He went straight off to the magistrate and gave himself up. "You have no accuser," said the astonished official, "yet you accuse yourself. We have no law in Korea to meet your case." So he dismissed him.

One of the missionaries declared, "It paid well to have spent several months in prayer, for when God gave the Holy Spirit, He accomplished more in half a day than all the missionaries together could have accomplished in half a year." In less than two months, more than two thousand heathen were converted. The burning zeal of those converts has become a byword. Some of them gave all they had to build a church and wept when they could not give more. They realized the power of prayer. Those converts were baptized with the "Spirit of supplication." In one church it was announced that a daily prayer meeting would be held at 4:30 every morning. The very first day four hundred people arrived long before the stated hour, eager to pray. The number rapidly increased to six hundred, as days went on. At Seoul, eleven hundred is the average attendance at the weekly prayer meeting.

Heathen people came to see what was happening. They exclaimed in astonishment, "The living God is among you!" Those poor heathen saw what many Christians fail to see. Did not Christ say, *For where two or three are gathered together in my name, there am I in the midst of them* (Matt. 18:20)? What is possible in Korea is possible here. God is no respecter of nations. He is longing to bless us, longing to pour His Spirit upon us.

Now, if we here in this so-called Christian country really believed in prayer, in our Lord's own gracious promises, should we avoid prayer meetings? If we had any genuine concern for the lost condition of thousands in our own land

and tens of thousands in heathen lands, should we withhold our prayers? Surely we do not think so, or we would pray more. "Ask of Me; I will give," says an almighty, all-loving God, and we scarcely heed His words.

Truly, converts from heathendom put us to shame. In my journeys, I came to Rawalpindi in northwest India. What do you think happened there? Some of Pandita Ramabai's girls camped there. But a little while before this, Pandita Ramabai had said to her girls, "If there is any blessing in India, we may have it. Let us ask God to tell us what we must do in order to have the blessing."

As she read her Bible she paused over the verses that said, *wait for the promise of the Father, … ye shall receive the virtue of the Holy Spirit which shall come upon you* (Acts 1:4-8). "Wait. Why, we have never done this!" she cried. "We have prayed, but we have never expected any greater blessing today than we had yesterday." Oh, how they prayed. One prayer meeting lasted six hours. And what a marvelous blessing God poured out in answer to their prayers.

While some of these girls were at Rawalpindi, a lady missionary, looking out of her tent about midnight, was surprised to see a light burning in one of the girls' tents – a thing quite contrary to rules. She went to protest, but found the youngest of those ten girls, a child of fifteen, kneeling in the farthest corner of the tent, holding a little tallow candle in one hand and a list of names for intercession in the other. She had five hundred names on her list – five hundred of the fifteen hundred girls in Pandita Ramabai's school. Hour after hour she was naming them before God. No wonder God's blessing fell wherever those girls went and upon whomever those girls prayed for.

Pastor Ding Li Mei of China has the names of eleven hundred students on his prayer list. Many hundreds have been won to Christ through his prayers. And so genuine are his converts that many scores of them have entered the Christian ministry.

It would be an easy matter to add to these amazing and inspiring stories of blessing through prayer. But there is no need to do so. I know that God wants me to pray. I know that God wants you to pray.

"If there is any blessing in England, we may have it." Nay, if there is any blessing in Christ, we may have it. *Blessed be the God and Father of our Lord Jesus Christ, who has blessed us with all spiritual blessings in heavenly things in Christ* (Eph. 1:3).

Prayer is the key, and faith turns the key, opens the door, and claims the blessing.

God's great storehouse is full of blessings. Only prayer can unlock that storehouse. Prayer is the key, and faith turns the key, opens the door, and claims the blessing. *Blessed are the pure in heart, for they shall see God.* And to see Him is to pray aright.

Listen. We have come, you and I, once more to the parting of the ways. All our past failure, all our past inefficiency and insufficiency, and all our past unfruitfulness in service can be banished now, once and for all, if we will give prayer its proper place. Do it today. Do not wait for a more convenient time.

Everything worth having depends upon the decision we make. Truly, God is a wonderful God. And one of the most wonderful things about Him is that He puts His all at the disposal of the prayer of faith. Believing prayer from a wholly cleansed heart never fails. God has given us His word for it. Yet vastly more extraordinary is the amazing fact that Christian men and women should either not believe God's word or fail to put it to the test.

When Christ is "all in all," when He is Savior and Lord and King of our whole being, then He is the One who prays our prayers. We can then truthfully alter one word of a well-known verse and say that the Lord Jesus ever liveth to make intercession *in* us. Oh, that we might make the Lord Jesus *marvel* not at our unbelief but at our faith. When our Lord shall again *marvel*, and say of us, *Verily I say unto you that not even in Israel have I found such faith* (Matt. 8:10), then indeed shall "palsy" paralysis be transformed into power.

Has not our Lord come to *cast fire* upon us? Are we *already kindled*? Can He not use us as much as He used those mere children of Khedgaon, India? God is no respecter of persons. If we can humbly and truthfully say, *For to me to live is Christ* (Phil. 1:21), will He not manifest forth His mighty power in us?

Some of us have been reading about Praying Hyde. Truly, his intercession changed things. Men tell us that they were thrilled when John Hyde prayed. They were stirred to their inmost being when he just pleaded the name, "Jesus, Jesus, Jesus," and a baptism of love and power came upon them.

But it was not John Hyde; it was the Holy Spirit of God whom one consecrated man, filled with that Spirit, brought down upon all around him. May we not all become "Praying Hydes"? Do you say, "No. He had a special gift of prayer"? Very well, how did he get it? He was once just an ordinary Christian man like any of us.

Have you noticed that, humanly speaking, he owed his prayer life to the prayers of his father's friend? Understand this point. It is one of greatest importance and one which may profoundly affect your whole life. Perhaps I may be allowed to tell the story fully, for so much depends upon it. Shall we quote John Hyde himself? He was on board a ship sailing for India, where he was going as a missionary.

He says, "My father had a friend who greatly desired to be a foreign missionary, but was not permitted to go. This friend wrote me a letter directed in care of the ship. I received it a few hours out of New York harbor. The words were not many, but the essence of them was this: 'I shall not cease praying for you, dear John, until you are filled with the Holy Spirit.' When I had read the letter, I crumpled it up in anger and threw it on the deck. Did this friend think I had not received the baptism of the Spirit, or that I would think of going to India without this equipment? I was angry.

"But by and by better judgment prevailed, and I picked up the letter, and read it again. Possibly, I did need something, which I had not yet received. I paced up and down the deck, a battle raging within. I felt uncomfortable: I loved the writer; I knew the holy life he lived, and down in my heart there was a conviction that he was right, and that I was not fit to be a missionary ... This went on for two or three days, until I felt perfectly miserable ... At last, in a kind of despair, I asked the Lord to fill me with the Holy Spirit; and the moment I did this, I began to see myself and what a selfish ambition I had."

But he did not yet receive the blessing sought. He landed in India and went with a fellow missionary to an open-air service. "The missionary spoke," said John Hyde, "and I was told that he was speaking about Jesus Christ as the real Savior from sin. When he had finished his address, a respectable-looking man, speaking good English, asked the missionary whether he himself had been thus saved. The question went home to my heart; for if it had been asked of me, I would have had to confess that Christ had not fully saved me, because I knew there was a sin in my life, which had not been taken away. I realized what a dishonor it would be on the name of Christ to have to confess that I was preaching a Christ who had not delivered me from sin, though I was proclaiming to others that He was a perfect Savior. I went back to my room, shut myself in, and told the Lord that it must be one of two things: either He must give me victory over all my sins, and especially over the sin that so easily beset me, or I must return to America and seek some other work. I said I could not stand up to preach the gospel until I could testify of its power in my own life.

"I realized how reasonable this was, and the Lord assured me that He was able and willing to deliver me from all sin. He did deliver me, and I have not had a doubt of this since." It was then, and then only, that John Hyde became Praying Hyde. And it is only by such a full surrender and such a definite claiming to be delivered from the power of sin in our lives that you and I can be people of prevailing prayer. The point we wish to emphasize, however, is the one already mentioned. A comparatively unknown man prays for John Hyde, who was then unknown to the world, and by his prayers he brings down such a blessing upon him that everyone knows of him now as Praying Hyde.

Did you say in your heart, dear reader, a little while ago, that you could not hope to be a Praying Hyde? Of course, we cannot all give so much time to prayer. For physical or other reasons we may be hindered from long continued praying. But we may all have his spirit of prayer. And may we not all do for others what the unnamed friend did for John Hyde?

Can we not pray the blessing down upon others? Upon your pastor? Upon your friend? Upon your family? What a ministry is ours, if we will but enter it. But to do so, we must make the full surrender, which John Hyde made.

Failure in prayer is due to fault in the heart.

Have we done it? Failure in prayer is due to fault in the heart. Only the *pure in heart* can see God. And only those who *call on the Lord out of a pure heart* can confidently claim answers to their prayers (2 Tim. 2:22).

What a revival would break out; what a mighty blessing would come down, if only everyone who read these words would claim the fullness of the Holy Spirit now.

Do you not see why it is that God wants us to pray? Do you now see why everything worth having depends upon prayer? There are several reasons, but one stands out clearly and vividly before us after reading this chapter. It is just this: If we ask and God does not give, then the fault is with us. Every unanswered prayer is a clarion call to search the heart to see what is wrong there; for the promise is unmistakable in its clearness: *If ye ask any thing in my name, I will do it* (John 14:14).

Truly, he who prays puts, not God, but his own spiritual life to the test.

> Let me come closer to Thee, Jesus.
>   Oh, closer every day;
> Let me lean harder on Thee, Jesus.
>   Yea, harder all the way.

CHAPTER 4

ASKING FOR SIGNS

D oes God indeed answer prayer?" is a question often on the lips of people, and more often still in their inmost hearts. "Is prayer of any real use?" Somehow or other we cannot help praying; but then even pagan savages cry out to someone or something to aid them in times of danger and disaster and distress.

And those of us who really do believe in prayer are soon faced with another question: "Is it right to put God to the test?" Moreover, a further thought flashes into our minds: "Dare we put God to the test?" For there is little doubt that failure in the prayer life is often always due to failure in the spiritual life. So many people harbor much unbelief in the heart regarding the value and effectiveness of prayer; and without faith, prayer is vain.

Asking for signs? Putting God to the test? Would to God we could persuade Christian men and women to do so. Why, what a test this would be of our own faith in God and of our own holiness of life. Prayer is the touchstone of true godliness. God asks our prayers, values our prayers, demands our prayers. And if those prayers fail, we have only ourselves to blame. We do not mean by this that effective prayer always gets just what it asks for. The Bible teaches us that we are allowed to put God to the test. The example of Gideon in Old Testament days is sufficient to show us that God honors our faith even when that faith is faltering. He allows us to "prove Him" even after a definite promise from Himself. This is a very great comfort to us.

And Gideon said unto God, Wilt thou save Israel by my hand as thou hast said? Behold, I will put a fleece of wool in the threshing floor; and if the dew is on the fleece only ... then shall I know that thou wilt save Israel by my hand as thou hast said. Yet, although there was a *bowl full of water* in the fleece the next morning, this did not satisfy Gideon. He dared to put God to the test the second time and to ask that the fleece should be dry instead of wet the following night. *And God did so that night* (Judges 6:36-40).

The almighty God doing what a hesitating man asks Him to do is very wonderful. We catch our breath and stand amazed, scarcely knowing which startles us more – the daring of the man or the condescension of God. Of course, there is more in the story than meets the eye. No doubt Gideon thought that the fleece represented himself.

If God would indeed fill him with His Spirit, his salvation was assured. But as he wrung the fleece out, he began to compare himself with the saturated wool. "How unlike this fleece I am. God promises deliverance, but I do not feel full of the Spirit of God. No inflow of the mighty power of God seems to have come into me. Am I indeed fit for this great feat?"

No. But then, it is "Not I, but God."

"O God, let the fleece be dry – canst Thou still work?

Even if I do not feel any superhuman power, any fullness of spiritual blessing within me; even if I feel as dry as this fleece, canst Thou still deliver Israel by my arm?" (Little wonder that he prefaced his prayer with the words, *Let not thine anger be hot against me.*) *And God did so that night for it was dry upon the fleece only, and there was dew on all the ground* (Judges 6:40).

Yes, there is more in the story than can be seen at a glance. And is it not so in our own case? The Devil so often assures us that our prayers cannot claim an answer because of the "dryness" of our souls. Answers to prayer, however, do not depend upon our feelings, but upon the trustworthiness of the Promiser.

...is God not grieved when we doubt His goodness?

Now, we are not urging that Gideon's way of procedure is for us – or for anyone – the normal course of action. It seems to reveal much hesitation to believe God's Word. In fact, it looks gravely like doubting God. And is God not grieved when we doubt His goodness?

The higher and better and safer way is to "ask, nothing doubting." But it is very comforting and assuring to us to know that God allowed Gideon to put Him to the test. Nor is this the only such case mentioned in Scripture. The most surprising instance of "proving God" happened on the Sea of Galilee. The apostle Peter put our Lord Himself to the test: "*Lord if it be Thou,*" yet our Savior had already said, "*Trust that I AM*" ... *if it be thou, bid me to come unto thee upon the water. And he said, Come. And when Peter was come down out of the ship, he walked upon the water* (Matt. 14:27-29). But this "testing faith" of Peter's soon failed him. *Little faith* (v. 31) so often and so quickly becomes "doubt."

Remember that Christ did not reprove him for coming. Our Lord did not say, "Wherefore didst thou come?" but "Wherefore didst thou doubt?"

To put God to the test is, after all, not the best method. He has given us so many promises contingent on believing prayer, and has so often proved His power and His willingness to answer prayer, that we ought to hesitate before we ask Him for signs and wonders.

But, someone may be thinking, does not the Lord God Almighty Himself bid us to put Him to the test? Did He not say, *Bring ye all the tithes into the storehouse, … and prove me now in this, said the* LORD *of the hosts, if I will not open you the windows of heaven and pour you out a blessing that there shall not be room enough to receive it* (Mal. 3:10)?

Yes, that is true: God does say, "Prove Me; test Me." But we are the ones who are thus tested. If the *windows of heaven* are not opened when we pray, and this blessing of fullness to overflowing is not bestowed upon us, it can only be because we are not whole tithers. When we are totally yielded to God and have brought the whole tithe into the storehouse for God, we shall find such a blessing that we shall not need to put God to any test. We shall speak of this when we come to the question of unanswered prayer.

Meanwhile, we want every Christian to ask, "Have I ever fairly tested prayer?" How long has it been since you offered up a definite prayer? People pray for a blessing upon an address, or a meeting, or a mission; and some blessing is certain to come, for others are also pleading with God about the matter. You ask for relief from pain or healing of sickness, but godless people, for whom no one appears to be praying, often recover, and sometimes in a seemingly miraculous way. And we may feel that we might have recovered even if no prayer had been offered on our behalf. It seems to me that many people cannot put their finger upon any really definite and conclusive answer to prayer in their own experience. Most Christians do not give God a chance to show His delight in granting His children's petitions, for their requests are vague and indefinite. If this is so, it is not surprising that prayer is often a mere form, an almost mechanical repetition, day by day, of certain phrases; a few minutes of exercise, morning and evening.

Then there is another point. When in prayer, have you ever had the witness affirm that your request was granted? Those who know something of the private life of people of prayer are often amazed at the complete assurance, which comes over them at times, that their prayers are answered, long before the blessing they seek is actually in their possession. One prayer warrior would say, "A peace came over my soul. I was confident my request was granted to me." He then thanked God for what he was quite sure God had done for him, and his assurance would prove to be absolutely well founded.

Our Lord Himself always had this assurance, and we should bear in mind that, although He was God, He lived His earthly life as a perfect Man, depending upon the Holy Spirit of God.

When He stood before the opened tomb of Lazarus, before He had actually called upon the dead to come forth, He said, *Father, I thank thee that thou hast heard Me. And I knew that thou hearest me always.* Why, then, did He utter His thanks? *Because of the people who stand by I said it, that they may believe that thou hast sent me* (John 11:41-42). If

Christ is dwelling in our hearts by faith, and the Holy Spirit is breathing into us our petitions as we are *praying in the Holy Spirit*, shouldn't we know that the Father hears us? (Jude 20). And won't those who stand by begin to recognize that we too are God-sent?

Men of prayer and women of prayer will agonize before God for something, which they know is according to His will, because of some definite promise on the page of Scripture. They may pray for hours, or even for days, when suddenly the Holy Spirit reveals to them in no uncertain way that God has granted their request, and they are confident that they don't need to send up any more petitions to God about the matter. It is as if God said in a clear voice, "Thy prayer is heard and I have granted thee the desire of thy heart." This is not the experience of only one person, but most people to whom prayer is the basis of their life will bear witness to the same fact. Nor is it a solitary experience in their lives; it occurs again and again.

...prayer must give place to action.

Then prayer must give place to action. God taught Moses this: *Why criest thou unto me? Speak unto the sons of Israel that they go forward* (Ex. 14:15).

We are not surprised to find that Dr. Goforth, a missionary in China, has this assurance given to him that his petitions are granted. "I knew that God had answered. I received definite assurance that He would open the way." Why should anyone be surprised at this? The Lord Jesus said, *Ye are my friends if ye do whatsoever I command you. From now on I do not call you slaves, for the slave does not know what his lord does; but I have called you friends* (John 15:14-15). Are you surprised, then, if the Lord lets us, His friends, know something of His plans and purposes?

The question at once arises: Does God mean this to be the experience of only a few chosen saints, or does He wish all believers to exercise a like faith and have a like assurance that their prayers are answered?

We know that God is no respecter of persons, and therefore we know that any true believer in Him may share His mind and will. We are His friends if we do the things He commands us. One of those things is prayer. Our Savior begged His disciples to *have faith in God* (the literal translation is "have the faith of God"). Then, He declares, you can say to a mountain, *Remove thyself and cast thyself into the sea*, and if you believe and doubt not, it shall come to pass. Then He gives this promise: *Everything that ye ask for, praying, believe that ye receive it [in heaven], and it shall come upon you [on earth]* (Mark 11:24, author's addition). Now, this is exactly the experience we have been discussing. This is what real men and women of prayer do. Such things naturally escape the comprehension of unbelievers. Such things are perplexing to the half believers. Our Lord, however, desires that others should know that we are His disciples, sent as He was sent (John 17:18; 20:21). They will know this if we love one another (John 13:35). But another proof is provided, and it is this: if we know and they see that God heareth us always (John 11:42).

Some of us remember George Müller's wonderful prayer life. On one occasion, when crossing from Quebec to Liverpool, he had prayed that a chair he had written to New York for should arrive in time to catch the steamer, and he was quite confident that God had granted his petition. About half an hour before the tender was to take the passengers to the ship, the agents informed him that no chair had arrived, and it could not possibly come in time for the steamer. Now, Mrs. Müller suffered from seasickness, and it was absolutely essential that she have the chair. Yet nothing would induce Mr. Müller to buy another one from a shop nearby. "We have made special prayer that our heavenly Father would be pleased to provide it for us, and we will trust Him to do so" was his reply. He went on board absolutely sure that his trust was not misplaced and would not miscarry. Just before the tender left, a van drove up, and on the top of the load it carried was Mr. Müller's chair. It was hurried on board and placed into the hands of the very man who had urged George Müller to buy another one. When he handed it to Mr. Müller, the latter expressed no surprise, but quietly removed his hat and thanked his heavenly Father. To this man of God, such an answer to prayer was not wonderful, but natural. And don't you think that God allowed the chair to be held back till the very last minute as a lesson to Mr. Müller's friends and to us? We should never have heard of that incident but for that delay.

God does all He can to induce us to pray and to trust, and yet how slow we are to do so. Oh, what we miss through lack of faith and want of prayer. No one can have very real and deep communion with God who does not know how to pray so as to get answers to prayer.

If one has any doubt as to God's willingness to be put to the test, let him read a little book called *Nor Scrip* (Marshall, Morgan and Scott, Ltd.). Miss Amy Wilson Carmichael tells us in its pages how she repeatedly "proved God." One gets the impression from the book that it was no accident that led her to do so. Surely, God's hand was in it. For instance, in order to rescue a Hindu child from a life of "religious" shame, it was necessary to spend 100 rupees. Was she justified in doing so? She could help many girls for such a sum; should she spend it on one? Miss Wilson Carmichael felt led to pray that God would send her the round sum of 100 rupees – no more, no less – if it was His will that the money should be spent in this way. The exact amount of money came, and the sender explained that she sat down to write a check for a broken sum but had been compelled to make it 100 rupees.

That happened over fifteen years ago, and since that time this same missionary has tested God over and over, and He has never failed her. This is what she says: "Never once in fifteen years has a bill been left unpaid; never once has a man or woman been told when we were in need of help; but never once have we lacked any good thing. Once, as if to show what could be done if it were required, twenty-five pounds came by telegram. Sometimes a man would emerge from the clamoring crowd at a railway station and slip some indispensable gift of money into the hand, and be lost in the crowd again before the giver could be identified."

Is it wonderful? Wonderful. Why, what does the apostle John say, speaking by the Spirit of God? *And this is the confidence that we have in God, that, if we ask any thing according to his will, he hears us: And if we know that he hears us in whatever we ask, we also know that we have the petitions that we asked of him* (1 John 5:14-15). Have you and I such confidence? If not, why not?

To call it wonderful is to show our want of faith. It is natural to God to answer prayer – normal, not extraordinary. The fact is, let us be quite honest and straightforward about it: Many of us do not believe God. We may as well be quite candid about it. If we love God, we ought to pray, because He wants us to pray and commands us to pray. If we believe God, we shall pray because we cannot help doing so; we cannot get on without it. Fellow Christian, you believe in God, and you believe on Him (John 3:16), but have you advanced far enough in the Christian life to believe Him – that is, to believe what He says and all He says?

Doesn't it sound blasphemous to ask such a thing of a Christian? Yet how few believers really believe God. God forgive us. Has it ever struck you that we trust the word of our fellow man more easily than we trust God's word? And yet, when a man does "believe God," what miracles of grace God works in and through him! No man ever lived who has been revered and respected by so many peoples and tongues as that man of whom we are told three times over in the New Testament that *he believed God* (Rom. 4:3; Gal. 3:6; James 2:23). Yes, *Abraham believed God, and it was counted unto him for righteousness.* And today, Christian and Jew vie with each other in honoring his name. We implore every believer on Christ Jesus never to rest till he can say, *I believe God, that it shall be even as it was told me* (Acts 27:25).

But before we leave the question of testing God, we should point out that sometimes God leads us on to "prove Him." At times, God put it into the heart of Miss Wilson Carmichael to ask for things she saw no need for. Yet she felt compelled by the Holy Spirit to ask. Not only were they granted her, but they also proved an inestimable blessing. Yes, God knows what things we have need of, whether we want them or not, before we ask (Matt. 6:8).

The temptation would often come to Miss Wilson

Carmichael to let others know of some special need. But always the inner assurance would come, as in the very voice of God: "I know, and that is enough." And, of course, God was glorified.

During the trying days of the war, even the heathen used to say, "Their God feeds them."

"Is it not known all the country round," said a worldly heathen, "that your God hears prayer?"

Oh, what glory to God was brought about by their simple faith. Why don't we believe God? Why don't we take God at His word? Do believers or unbelievers ever say of us, "We know your prayers are answered"? Ye missionaries the wide world over, listen. (Oh, that these words might reach every ear and stir every heart.) It is the yearning desire of God – of our loving Savior Jesus Christ – that every one of us should have the same strong faith as that devoted lady missionary we were speaking about.

Do believers or unbelievers ever say of us, "We know your prayers are answered"?

Our loving Father does not wish any child of His to have one moment's anxiety or one unsatisfied need. No matter how great our need may be; no matter how numerous our requirements, if we only "prove Him" in the manner He bids us, we shall never have room enough to receive all the blessing He will give (Mal. 3:10).

> *Oh, what peace we often forfeit!*
> *Oh, what needless pain we bear!*
> *All because we do not carry*
> *Everything to God in prayer.[1]*

---

1   Joseph M. Scriven

Or, all because, when we do carry it, we do not believe God's word. Why is it we find it so hard to trust Him? Has He ever failed us? Has He not said over and over and over again that He will grant all petitions offered out of a pure heart, *in His name*? *Ask of Me*; *Pray ye*; *Prove Me*; *Try Me*. The Bible is full of answers to prayer – wonderful answers, miraculous answers – and yet somehow our faith fails us, and we dishonor God by distrusting Him.

> *If our faith were but more simple*
> *We should take Him at His word,*
> *And our lives would be all sunshine*
> *In the bounties of our Lord.*[2]

But our eye must be "single" if our faith is to be simple, and our *whole body shall be full of light* (Matt. 6:22). Christ must be the sole Master. We cannot expect to be free from anxiety if we are trying to serve God and mammon (Matt. 6:24-25). Again, we are led back to the victorious life. When we indeed present our bodies *in living sacrifice, holy, well pleasing unto God* (Rom. 12:1); when we present our members *to serve righteousness unto holiness* (Rom. 6:19); then He presents Himself to us and fills us with *all the fullness of God* (Eph. 3:19).

Let us ever bear in mind that real faith not only believes that God can, but that He does answer prayer. We may be slothful in prayer, but *the Lord is not late concerning His promise* (2 Peter 3:9). Is that not a striking expression?

Perhaps the most extraordinary testing of God, which another missionary tells, is the following: The question

---

2   Frederick William Faber

arose of purchasing a rest house in the hills nearby. Was it the right thing to do? Only God could decide. Much prayer was made. Eventually the petition was offered up that if it was God's will to purchase the house, the exact sum of 100 pounds should be received. That amount came at once. Yet they still hesitated. Two months later, they asked God to give them the same sign again of His approval of the purchase. That same day another check for 100 pounds came. Even after this, they scarcely wanted to proceed in the matter. In a few days' time, however, another round sum of 100 pounds was received, earmarked for the purchase of such a house.

Doesn't it flood our hearts with joy to remember that our gracious Savior is so kind? It is Luke the physician who tells us that God is kind (Luke 6:35). Love is always kind (1 Cor. 13:4); and God is love. Think over it when you pray. Our Lord is kind. It will help us in our intercessions. He patiently bears with us when our faith would falter. *How excellent is Thy mercy, O God* (Psalm 36:7); *thy mercy is better than life* (Psalm 63:3).

The danger is that we read of such simple faith in prayer and say, "How wonderful," and forget that God desires every one of us to have such faith and such prayer. God has no favorites. He wants me to pray; He wants you to pray. He allows such things to happen as we have described above and suffers them to come to our knowledge, not to surprise us, but to stimulate us. One sometimes wishes that Christian people would forget all the manmade rules with which we have hedged prayer about. Let us be simple. Let us be natural. Take God at His word. Let us remember that *the kindness and love of God our Savior toward man appeared* (Titus 3:4).

God sometimes leads us into the prayer life. Sometimes, however, God has to drive us into such a life.

As some of us look back over our comparatively prayerless life, what a thrill of wonder and of joy comes over us as we think of the kindness and *hope of Christ* (2 Thess. 3:5). Where would we have been without that? We fail Him, but, blessed be His name, He has never failed us, and He never will do so. We doubt Him; we mistrust His love and His providence and His guidance; we faint because of the way; we murmur because of the way; yet, all the time He is there blessing us and waiting to pour out a blessing on us so great that there shall not be room to receive it.

The promise of Christ still holds: *And whatsoever ye shall ask the Father in my name, that will I do, that the Father may be glorified in the Son* (John 14:13).

> *Prayer changes things – and yet how blind*
> *And slow we are to taste and see*
> *The blessedness that comes to those*
> *Who trust in Thee.*

But henceforth we will just believe God.

CHAPTER 5

WHAT IS PRAYER?

M r. D. L. Moody was once addressing a crowded meeting of children in Edinburgh. In order to get their attention, he began with a question: "What is prayer?" Looking for no reply, he expected to give the answer himself.

To his amazement, scores of little hands shot up all over the hall. He asked one lad to reply, and the answer came at once, clear and correct: "Prayer is an offering up of our desires unto God for things agreeable to His will, in the name of Christ, with confession of our sins and thankful acknowledgment of His mercies."

Mr. Moody's delighted comment was, "Thank God, my boy, that you were born in Scotland." But that was half a century ago. What sort of answer would he get today? How many English children could give a definition of prayer? Think for a moment and decide what answer you would give.

What do we mean by prayer? I believe the vast majority of Christians would say, "Prayer is asking things from God." But surely prayer is much more than "getting God to run our errands for us," as someone puts it. It is a higher thing than the beggar knocking at the rich man's door.

The word *prayer* really means "a wish directed towards," that is, towards God. All that true prayer seeks is God Himself, for with Him we get all we need. Prayer is simply "the turning of the soul to God." David describes it as the lifting up of the living soul to the living God. *Unto Thee, O Lord, do I lift up my soul* (Psalm 25:1). What a beautiful description of prayer that is. When we desire the Lord Jesus to behold our souls, we also desire that the beauty of holiness may be upon us.

When we lift up our souls to God in prayer, it gives God an opportunity to do what He will in us and with us. It is putting ourselves at God's disposal. God is always on our side, but we are not always on His side. When man prays, we give God the opportunity.

> *Prayer is the soul's sincere desire,*
> *Uttered or expressed,*
> *The motion of a hidden fire*
> *That trembles in the breast.*[3]

"Prayer," says an old Jewish mystic, "is the moment when heaven and earth kiss each other."

Prayer, then, is certainly not persuading God to do what we want Him to do. It is not bending the will of a reluctant God to our will. It does not change His purpose, although it may release His power. "We must not conceive of prayer as overcoming God's reluctance," says Archbishop Richard Trench, "but as laying hold of His highest willingness."

For God always purposes our greatest good. Even the prayer offered in ignorance and blindness cannot swerve

---

3   James Montgomery

Him from that, although, when we persistently pray for some harmful thing, our willfulness may bring it about, and we suffer accordingly. *And he gave them their request*, says the psalmist, *but sent leanness into their soul* (Psalm 106:15). They brought this *leanness* upon themselves. They were "cursed with the burden of a granted prayer."

Prayer, in the minds of some people, is only for emergencies. Danger threatens, sickness comes, things are lacking, difficulties arise, and then they pray. Like the infidel down in a coal mine: when the roof began falling, he began praying. An old Christian standing by quietly remarked, "Aye, there's nothing like cobs of coal to make a man pray."

Prayer is much more than merely asking God for something...

Prayer is, however, much more than merely asking God for something, although that is a very valuable part of prayer, if only because it reminds us of our utter dependence upon God. It is also communion with God, intercourse with God, and talking with (not only to) God. We get to know people by talking with them. We get to know God in like manner. The highest result of prayer is not deliverance from evil or the securing of some thing, but knowledge of God. *And this is life eternal, that they might know thee the only true God* (John 17:3). Yes, prayer discovers more of God, and that is the soul's greatest discovery. Men still cry out, *Oh, that I knew where I might find him! that I might come even to His seat!* (Job 23:3).

The kneeling Christian always "finds" Him and is found of Him. The heavenly vision of the Lord Jesus blinded the eyes of Saul of Tarsus on his downward course, but he tells us, later on, that when he was praying in the temple at Jerusalem, he fell into a trance and *saw him* (Jesus) (Acts

22:18). Then it was that Christ gave him his great commission to go to the Gentiles. Vision is always a precursor of vocation and venture. It was so with Isaiah. *I saw the Lord sitting upon a throne, high and lifted up, and his train filled the temple* (Isa. 6:1). The prophet was evidently in the sanctuary praying when this happened. This vision also was a prelude to a call to service: *Go and tell ...* Now, we cannot get a vision of God unless we pray. And where there is no vision the soul perishes.

A vision of God! Brother Lawrence once said, "Prayer is nothing else than a sense of God's presence," and that is just the practice of the presence of God.

A friend of Horace Bushnell was present when that man of God prayed. There came over him a wonderful sense of God's nearness. He says, "When Horace Bushnell buried his face in his hands and prayed, I was afraid to stretch out my hand in the darkness, lest I should touch God." Was the psalmist of old conscious of such a thought when he cried, *My soul, rest thou only in God* (Psalm 62:5)? I believe that much of our failure in prayer is due to the fact that we have not looked into this question, "What is prayer?" It is good to be conscious that we are always in the presence of God. It is better to gaze upon Him in adoration. But it is best of all to commune with Him as a Friend, and that is prayer.

Real prayer at its highest and best reveals a soul thirsting for God, just for God alone. Real prayer comes from the lips of those whose affection is set on things above. What a man of prayer Nicolaus Zinzendorf was. Why? He sought the Giver rather than His gifts. He said, "I have one passion: it is He, He alone." Even the Muslim seems to recognize this thought. He says that there are three degrees in prayer.

The lowest is that spoken only by the lips. The next is when, by a resolute effort, we succeed in fixing our thoughts on divine things. The third is when the soul finds it hard to turn away from God. Of course, we know that God bids us "ask" of Him. We all obey Him in this, and we may rest well assured that prayer both pleases God and supplies all our need. But he would be a strange child who only sought his father's presence when he desired some gift from him. And do we not all yearn to rise to a higher level of prayer than mere petition? How is it to be done?

It seems to me that only two steps are necessary, or shall we say two thoughts? There must be, first of all, a realization of God's glory and then of God's grace. We sometimes sing:

> Grace and glory flow from Thee;
> Shower, O shower them, Lord, on me.[4]

Nor is such a desire fanciful, although some may ask what God's glory has to do with prayer.

But shouldn't we remind ourselves Who He is to Whom we pray? There is logic in the couplet:

> Thou art coming to a King;
> Large petitions with thee bring.
> For his grace and power are such,
> None can ever ask too much.[5]

Do you think that any one of us spends enough time in pondering over, yes, and marveling over, God's exceedingly

---

4   Henry F. Lyte
5   John Newton

great glory? And do you suppose that any one of us has grasped the full meaning of the word *grace*? Aren't our prayers often ineffective and powerless and sometimes even prayerless, because we rush unthinkingly and unpreparedly into God's presence, without realizing the majesty and glory of the God Whom we are approaching, and without reflecting upon the exceedingly great riches of His glory in Christ Jesus, which we hope to draw upon? We must "think magnificently of God."

May we then suggest that before we lay our petitions before God, we first dwell in meditation upon His glory and His grace, for He offers us both. We must lift up the soul to God. Let us place ourselves, as it were, in the presence of God and direct our prayer to *the King of kings, and Lord of lords; the only one who has immortality, dwelling in the light which no man can approach unto, ... to whom be honour and power everlasting* (1 Tim. 6:15-16). Let us then give Him adoration and praise because of His exceedingly great glory. Consecration is not enough; there must be adoration.

Holy, holy, holy is the LORD of the hosts; cry the seraphim; *the whole earth is full of his glory* (Isa. 6:3). *Glory to God in the highest*, cries the whole *multitude of the heavenly host* (Luke 2:13-14). Yet some of us try to commune with God without stopping to *take off [our] shoes from [our] feet* (Ex. 3:5).

> *Lips cry "God be merciful"*
> *That ne'er cry "God be praised."*
>
> *O come let us adore Him!*

And we may approach His glory with boldness. Did not our Lord pray that His disciples might behold His glory (John 17:24)? Why? And why is *the whole earth full of his glory*? The telescope reveals His infinite glory. The microscope reveals His uttermost glory. Even the unaided eye sees surpassing glory in landscape, sunshine, sea, and sky. What does it all mean? These things are but a partial revelation of God's glory. It was not a desire for self-display that led our Lord to pray, *Father, … glorify thy Son, … O Father, glorify Thou Me* (John 17:1, 5 KJV). Our dear Lord wants us to realize His infinite trustworthiness and unlimited power, so that we can approach Him in simple faith and trust.

> *And we may approach His glory with boldness.*

In heralding the coming of Christ, the prophet declared that *the glory of the LORD shall be manifested, and all flesh shall see it together* (Isa. 40:5). Now, we must get a glimpse of that glory before we can pray aright. So our Lord said, *When ye pray, say, Our Father who art in the heavens [the realm of glory], Hallowed be thy name.* There is nothing like a glimpse of glory to banish fear and doubt. Before we offer up our petitions, wouldn't it help us to offer up our adoration in the words of praise used by some of the saints of old? Some devout souls may not need such help. We are told that Francis of Assisi would frequently spend an hour or two in prayer on the top of Mount Averno, while the only word that escaped his lips would be *God*, repeated at intervals. He began with adoration and often stopped there.

But most of us need some help to realize the glory of the invisible God, before we can adequately praise and adore Him. Old William Law said, "When you begin to pray, use expressions of the attributes of God that will make you sensible of His greatness and power."

This point is of such tremendous importance that we venture to remind our readers of helpful words. Some of us begin every day with a glance heavenwards while saying, "Glory be to the Father, and to the Son, and to the Holy Ghost." The prayer, "O Lord God most holy, O Lord most mighty, O holy and merciful Savior," is often enough to bring a solemn awe and a spirit of holy adoration upon the soul. The *Gloria in Excelsis Deo* of the communion service is most uplifting: "Glory be to God on high and in earth peace ... We praise Thee; we bless Thee; we worship Thee; we glorify Thee; we give thanks to Thee for Thy great glory, O Lord God, heavenly King, God the Father Almighty." Which of us can from the heart utter praise like that and remain unmoved or unconscious of the very presence and wondrous majesty of the Lord God Almighty? A verse of a hymn may serve the same purpose.

> *My God, how wonderful Thou art!*
> *Thy majesty how bright;*
> *How beautiful Thy mercy seat*
> *In depths of burning light!*
> *How wonderful, how beautiful,*
> *The sight of Thee must be;*
> *Thine endless wisdom, boundless power,*
> *And awful purity.*[6]

This carries us into the very heavenlies, as do the words:

---

6   Frederick W. Faber

Holy, holy, holy, Lord God Almighty,
  All Thy works shall praise Thy name
In earth, and sky, and sea.[7]

We need to cry out and to cry often, *My soul doth magnify the Lord, and my spirit hath rejoiced in God my Saviour* (Luke 1:46-47 KJV). Can we catch the spirit of the psalmist and sing, *Bless the LORD, O my soul, and all that is within me, bless the name of his holiness* (Psalm 103:1)? *Bless the LORD, O my soul. O LORD my God, thou art very great; thou art clothed with honour and majesty* (Psalm 104:1). When shall we learn that *in his temple every one speaks to his glory* (Psalm 29:9)? Let us too cry, "Glory!"

Such worship of God, such adoration and praise and thanksgiving, not only puts us into the spirit of prayer, but in some mysterious way, helps God work on our behalf. Do you remember those wonderful words, *Whosoever sacrifices praise glorifies me; and to him that orders his ways aright I will show the salvation of God* (Psalm 50:23)? Praise and thanksgiving not only open the gates of heaven for me to approach God, but also prepare a way for God to bless me. The apostle Paul cries, *Always rejoice*, before he says, *Pray without ceasing.* So then, our praise, as well as our prayers, are to be without ceasing.

At the raising of Lazarus, our Lord's prayer had as its first utterance a note of thanksgiving. *Father, I thank thee that thou hast heard me* (John 11:41). He said it for those around to hear. Yes, and for us to hear.

You may perhaps be wondering why it is that we should specially give thanks to God for His great glory when we

---

7   Reginald Heber

kneel in prayer, and why we should spend any time in thinking of and gazing upon that glory. But is He not the King of Glory? All He is and all He does is glory. His holiness is glorious (Ex. 15:11). His name is glorious (Deut. 28:58). His work is glorious (Psalm 111:3). His power is glorious (Col. 1:11). His voice is glorious (Isa. 30:30).

> *All things bright and beautiful,*
> *All creatures great and small.*
> *All things wise and wonderful,*
> *The Lord God made them all.*[8]

For of him and by him and in him are all things. To him be the glory for the ages (Rom. 11:36). And this is the God who bids us come to Him in prayer. This God is our God, and He has *gifts for men* (Psalm 68:18). God says that everyone that is called by His name has *This God is our God* been created for His glory (Isa. 43:7). His church is to be a glorious church holy and without blemish (Eph. 5:27). Have you ever fully realized that the Lord Jesus desires to share with us the glory we see in Him? This is His great gift to you and me, His redeemed ones. Believe me, the more we have of God's glory, the less we shall seek His gifts. Not only in that day *when he shall come to be glorified in his saints* is there glory for us, but here and now today (2 Thess. 1:10). He wishes us to be partakers of His glory. Didn't our Lord Himself say so? *And the glory which thou gavest me I have given them*, He declares (John 17:22 KJV). What is God's command? *Arise, shine; for thy light is come, and the glory of the LORD is risen upon thee.*

---

8   Cecil F. Alexander

Nay, more than this: *His glory shall be seen upon thee*, says the inspired prophet (Isa. 60:1-2).

God would have people say of us as Peter said of the disciples of old: *For the glory and the Spirit of God rests upon you* (1 Peter 4:14). Wouldn't that be an answer to most of our prayers? Could we ask for anything better? How can we get this glory? How are we to reflect it? Only as the result of prayer. It is when we pray, that the Holy Spirit takes of the things of Christ and reveals them unto us (John 16:15).

It was when Moses prayed, *I beseech thee, show me thy glory*, that he not only saw somewhat of it, but also shared something of that glory, and his own face shone with the light of it (Ex. 33:18; 34:29). And when we too gaze upon *the glory of God in the face of Jesus Christ* (2 Cor. 4:6 KJV), we shall see not only a glimpse of that glory, but we shall also gain something of it ourselves.

Now, that is prayer and the highest result of prayer. Nor is there any other way of securing that glory, that God may be glorified in us (Isa. 60:21).

Let us often meditate upon Christ's glory – gaze upon it and so reflect it and receive it. This is what happened to our Lord's first disciples. They said in awed tones, *We beheld his glory*. Yes, but what followed? A few plain, unlettered, obscure fishermen companied with Christ a little while, seeing His glory, and lo, they themselves caught something of that glory. And then others marveled and *took knowledge of them that they had been with Jesus* (Acts 4:13). And when we can declare with John, *truly our communion is with the Father and with his Son Jesus Christ* (1 John 1:3), people will say the same of us: "They have been with Jesus."

As we lift up our soul in prayer to the living God, we

gain the beauty of holiness as surely as a flower becomes beautiful by living in the sunlight. Wasn't our Lord Himself transfigured when He prayed? And the very fashion of our countenance will change, and we shall have our Mount of Transfiguration when prayer has its rightful place in our lives. And men will see in our faces the outward and visible sign of an inward and spiritual grace. Our value to God and to man is in exact proportion to the extent in which we reveal the glory of God to others.

What is prayer? It is a sign of spiritual life. I should as soon expect life in a dead man as spiritual life in a prayer-less soul. Our spirituality and our fruitfulness are always in proportion to the reality of our prayers. If we have at all wandered away from home in the matter of prayer, let us today resolve, *I will arise and go to my father and will say unto him, Father* (Luke 15:18).

At this point I laid down my pen, and on the page of the first paper I picked up were these words: "The secret of failure is that we see men rather than God. Romanism trembled when Martin Luther saw God. The Great Awakening sprang into being when Jonathan Edwards saw God. The world became the parish of one man when John Wesley saw God. Multitudes were saved when Whitfield saw God. Thousands of orphans were fed when George Müller saw God. And He is *the same yesterday, today, and forever.*"

Isn't it time that we got a new vision of God in all His glory? Who can say what will happen when the church sees God? But let us not wait for others. Let us, each one for himself, with unveiled face and unsullied heart, get this vision of the glory of the Lord.

Blessed are the pure in heart, for they shall see God (Matt.

5:8). No missionary whom it has been my joy to meet ever impressed me quite as much as Dr. Wilbur Chapman. He wrote to a friend:

I have learned some great lessons concerning prayer. At one of our missions in England, the audiences were exceedingly small. But I received a note saying that an American missionary … was going to pray God's blessing down upon our work. He was known as 'Praying Hyde.' Almost instantly the tide turned. The hall became packed, and at my first invitation, fifty men accepted Christ as their Savior. As we were leaving, I said, 'Mr. Hyde, I want you to pray for me.' He came to my room, turned the key in the door, dropped on his knees, and waited five minutes without a single syllable coming from his lips. I could hear my own heart thumping and his beating. I felt the hot tears running down my face. I knew I was with God. Then, with upturned face, down which the tears were streaming, he said, 'O God.' Then for five minutes at least, he was still again; and then, when he knew that he was talking with God … there came up from the depth of his heart such petitions for men as I had never heard before. I rose from my knees to know what real prayer was. We believe that prayer is mighty, and we believe it as we never did before.

Dr. Chapman used to say, "It was a season of prayer with John Hyde that made me realize what real prayer was. I owe to him more than I owe to any man for showing me what a prayer life is and what a real consecrated life is. Jesus Christ became a new Ideal to me, and I had a glimpse of His prayer life; and I had a longing which has remained to this day to be a real praying man." And God the Holy Spirit can teach us.

Oh, ye who sigh and languish
*   And mourn your lack of power,*
Hear ye this gentle whisper:
*   "Could ye not watch one hour?"*
For fruitfulness and blessing
*   There is no royal road;*
The power for holy service
*   Is intercourse with God.*[9]

---

9   John Hyde

CHAPTER 6

HOW SHALL I PRAY?

H ow shall I pray? Could there be a more important
question for a Christian to ask? How shall I approach
the King of Glory?

When we read Christ's promises regarding prayer, we
are apt to think that He puts far too great a power into our
hands, unless, indeed, we hastily conclude that it is impossible for Him to act as He promises. He says, ask *anything*,
whatsoever, what ye will, and it shall be done.

But then He puts in a qualifying phrase. He says that
we are to ask in His name. That is the condition, and the
only one, although, as we shall remind ourselves later, it is
sometimes couched in different words.

If, therefore, we ask and do not receive, it can only be
that we are not fulfilling this condition. If, then, we are
true disciples of His, if we are sincere, we shall take pains
(infinite pains, if need be) to discover just what it means
to ask in His name; and we shall not rest content until we
have fulfilled that condition. Let us read the promise again
to be quite sure about it. *And whatsoever ye shall ask the
Father in my name, that will I do, that the Father may be*

glorified in the Son. If ye ask any thing in my name, I will do it (John 14:13-14).

This was something quite new, for our Lord said so. *Until now ye have asked nothing in my name; ask, and ye shall receive, that your joy may be fulfilled* (John 16:24).

Five times over our Lord repeats this simple condition, *in my name* (John 14:13-14; 15:16; 16:23-24, 26). Evidently, something very important is implied here. It is more than a condition; it is also a promise, an encouragement, for our Lord's biddings are always His enablings. What, then, does it mean to ask in His name? We must know this at all costs, for it is the secret of all power in prayer. And it is possible to make a wrong use of those words. Our Lord said, *For many shall come in my name, saying, I am Christ, and shall deceive many* (Matt. 24:5). He might well have said, "And many shall think they are praying to the Father in my name, while deceiving themselves."

> *And many shall think they are praying to the Father in my name, while deceiving themselves*

Does it mean just adding the words, "and all this we ask in the name of Jesus Christ," at the end of our prayers?

Many people apparently think that it does. But have you never heard nor offered prayers full of self-will and selfishness, which ended up in that way, "for Christ's sake. Amen"?

God could not answer the prayers James refers to in his epistle because those who offered them added, "we ask these things in the name of our Lord Jesus Christ." Those Christians were asking *amiss* (James 4:3). A wrong prayer cannot be made right by the addition of some mystic phrase.

And a right prayer does not fail if some such words are omitted. No, it is more than a question of words. Our Lord is thinking about faith and facts more than about some formula. The chief object of prayer is to glorify the Lord Jesus. We are to ask in Christ's name *that the Father may be glorified in the Son* (John 14:13).

Listen. We are not to seek wealth or health, prosperity or success, ease or comfort, spirituality or fruitfulness in service simply for our own enjoyment, advancement, or popularity, but only for Christ's sake for His glory. Let us take three steps to a right understanding of those important words, *in my name.*

(1) There is a sense in which some things are done only "for Christ's sake" because of His atoning death. Those who do not believe in the atoning death of Christ cannot pray *in His name.* They may use the words, but without effect. For we are *justified in his blood* (Rom. 5:9), and *we have redemption through his blood, the forgiveness of sins* (Eph. 1:7; Col. 1:14). In these days, when Unitarianism under its guileful name of Modernism has invaded all sects, it is most important to remember the place and work of the shed blood of Christ, or "prayer" becomes a delusion and a snare.

Let us illustrate this point by an experience which happened quite early in Mr. Moody's ministry. The wife of an infidel judge, a man of great intellectual gifts, begged Mr. Moody to speak to her husband. Moody, however, hesitated at arguing with such a man and told him so quite frankly. "But," he added, "if ever you are converted, will you promise to let me know?"

The judge laughed cynically and replied, "Oh, yes, I'll let you know quick enough if I am ever converted." Moody went his way, relying upon prayer. That judge was converted

– and within a year. He kept his promise and told Moody just how it came about.

I began to grow very uneasy and miserable one night when my wife was at a prayer meeting. I went to bed before she came home. I could not sleep all that night. Getting up early the next morning, I told my wife I should not need any breakfast and went off to my office. Telling the clerks they could take a holiday, I shut myself up in my private room. But I became more and more wretched. Finally, I fell on my knees and asked God to forgive me my sins, but I would not say 'for Jesus' sake,' for I was Unitarian, and I did not believe in the atonement. In an agony of mind I kept praying, 'O God, forgive me my sins,' but no answer came. At last, in desperation, I cried, 'O God, for Christ's sake forgive my sins.' Then I found peace at once.

That judge had no access to the presence of God until he sought it in the name of Jesus Christ. When he came in Christ's name, he was at once heard and forgiven. Yes, to pray *in the name* of the Lord Jesus is to ask for things, which the blood of Christ has secured – "purchased" – for us. We have *boldness to enter into the sanctuary by the blood of Jesus* (Heb. 10:19). There is entrance by no other way.

But this is not all that those words, *in my name*, mean.

(2) The most familiar illustration of coming *in the name* of Christ is that of drawing money from a bank by means of a check. I can draw from my bank account only up to the amount of my deposit there. In my own name, I can go no further. In the Bank of England, I have no money whatsoever and can therefore draw nothing from there. But suppose a very wealthy man who has a big account there gives me a blank check bearing his signature and bids me

fill it in to any amount I choose. He is my friend. What shall I do? Shall I just satisfy my present need, or shall I draw as much as I dare? I shall certainly do nothing to offend my friend or to lower myself in his esteem.

Well, we are told by some that heaven is our bank. God is the Great Banker, for *every good gift and every perfect gift is from above and comes down from the Father* (James 1:17). We need a "check" wherewith to "draw" upon this boundless store. The Lord Jesus gives us a blank check in prayer. "Fill it in," says He, "to any amount; ask 'anything,' 'what ye will,' and you shall have it. Present your check in My name, and your request will be honored." Let me put this in the words of a wellknown evangelist of today: "That is what happens when I go to the bank of heaven, when I go to God in prayer. I have nothing deposited there; I have no credit there; and if I go in my own name, I will get absolutely nothing. But Jesus Christ has unlimited credit in heaven, and He has granted me the privilege of going with His name on my checks; and when I thus go, my prayers will be honored to any extent. To pray, then, in the name of Christ is to pray, not on the ground of my credit, but His."

This is all very delightful and, in a sense, very true.

If the check were drawn on a government account or upon some wealthy corporation, one might be tempted to get all one could. But remember, we are coming to a loving Father to Whom we owe everything, and Whom we love with all our heart, and to Whom we may come repeatedly. In cashing our checks at the bank of heaven, we desire chiefly His honor and His glory. We wish to do only that which is pleasing in His sight. To cash some of our "checks," to answer some of our prayers, would only bring dishonor to His name and discredit and discomfort to us. True, His resources are unlimited; but His honor is assailable.

But experience makes argument unnecessary. Dear reader, haven't we all tried this method only to fail?

How many of us dare say we have never come away from the bank of heaven without getting what we asked for, although we have apparently asked *in Christ's name?* Wherein do we fail? Is it because we do not seek to learn God's will for us? We must not try to exceed His will.

We must not try to exceed His will.

May I give a personal experience of my own which has never been told in public and which is probably quite unique? It happened over thirty years ago, and now I see why. It makes such a splendid illustration of what we are now trying to learn about prayer.

A well-to-do friend, and an exceedingly busy one, wished to give me one pound towards a certain object. He invited me to his office and hastily wrote out a check for the amount. He folded the check and handed it to me, saying, "I will not cross[10] it. Will you kindly cash it at the bank?" On arriving at the bank, I glanced at my name on the check without troubling to verify the amount, endorsed it, and handed it to a clerk. "This is rather a big sum to cash over the counter," he said, eyeing me narrowly.

"Yes," I replied laughingly, "one pound."

"No," said the clerk, "this is made out for one thousand pounds."

And so it was. My friend was, no doubt, accustomed to writing big checks; and he had actually written "one thousand" instead of "one" pound. Now, what was my position

---

10   A crossed check must be deposited into an account, it cannot be cashed.

legally? The check was truly in his name. The signature was all right. My endorsement was all right. Could I not demand the one thousand pounds, provided there was sufficient in the account? The check was written deliberately, if hurriedly, and freely to me – why should I not take the gift? Why not?

But I was dealing with a friend, a generous friend, to whom I owed many deeds of lovingkindness. He had revealed his mind to me. I knew his wishes and desires.

He meant to give me one pound, and no more. I knew his intention, his mind, and at once took back the all-too-generous check, and in due time I received just one pound, according to his will. Had that donor given me a blank check, the result would have been exactly the same. He would have expected me to write in "one pound," and my honor would have been at stake in my doing so. Need we draw the lesson? God has His will for each one of us, and unless we seek to know that will, we are likely to ask for "a thousand," when He knows that "one" will be best for us. In our prayers we are coming to a Friend, a loving Father. We owe everything to Him. He bids us come to Him whenever we like for all we need. His resources are infinite.

But He bids us to remember that we should ask only for those things that are according to His will, only for that which will bring glory to His name. John says, *if we ask any thing according to his will, he hears us* (1 John 5:14). So then our Friend gives us a blank check, and leaves us to fill in anything; but He knows that if we truly love Him, we shall never put down, never ask for, things He is not willing to give us, because they would be harmful to us.

Perhaps with most of us the fault lies in the other

direction. God gives us a blank check and says, "Ask for a pound," and we ask for a shilling (twenty shillings equals one pound). Would not my friend have been insulted had I treated him thus? Do we ask enough? Do we dare to ask *according to his riches in glory*?

The point we are dwelling upon, however, is this – we cannot be sure that we are praying *in His name* unless we learn His will for us.

(3) But even now we have not exhausted the meaning of those words, *in my name*. We all know what it is to ask for a thing in the name of another. But we are very careful not to allow anyone to use our name who is not to be trusted, or he might abuse our trust and discredit our name. Gehazi, the trusted servant, dishonestly used Elisha's name when he ran after Naaman. In Elisha's name, he secured riches but also inherited a curse for his wickedness.

A trusted clerk often uses his employer's name and handles great sums of money as if they were his own. But he does this only as long as he is thought to be worthy of such confidence in him. And he uses the money for his master and not for himself. All our money belongs to our Master, Christ Jesus. We can go to God for supplies in His name, if we use all we get for His glory.

When I go to cash a check payable to me, the banker is quite satisfied if the signature of his client is genuine and I am the person authorized to receive the money. He does not ask for references to my character. He has no right whatever to enquire whether I am worthy to receive the money or to be trusted to use it aright. It is not so with the bank of heaven. Now, this is a point of greatest importance. Do not hurry over what is now to be said.

When I go to heaven's bank in the name of the Lord Jesus with a check drawn upon the unsearchable riches of Christ, God demands that I shall be a worthy recipient. Not "worthy" in the sense that I can merit or deserve anything from a holy God, but worthy in the sense that I am seeking the gift not for my own glory or self-interest, but only for the glory of God.

Otherwise, I may pray and not get. *Ye ask and receive not because ye ask amiss, that ye may consume it upon your pleasures* (James 4:3).

The great heavenly Banker will not cash checks for us if our motives are not right. Isn't this why so many fail in prayer? Christ's name is the revelation of His character. To pray *in His name* is to pray in His character, as His representative sent by Him. It is to pray by His Spirit and according to His will, to have His approval in our asking, to seek what He seeks, to ask help to do what He Himself would wish to be done, and to desire to do it, not for our own glorification but for His glory alone. To pray *in His name* we must have identity of interests and purpose. Self and its aims and desires must be entirely controlled by God's Holy Spirit, so that our wills are in complete harmony with Christ's will.

We must reach the attitude of Saint Augustine when he cried, "O Lord, grant that I may do Thy will as if it were my will, so that Thou mayest do my will as if it were Thy will."

Child of God, does this seem to make prayer *in His name* quite beyond us? That was not our Lord's intention. He is not mocking us. Speaking of the Holy Spirit, our Lord used these words: *the Comforter, ... whom the Father will send in my name* (John 14:26). Now, our Savior wants us to be so controlled by the Holy Spirit that we may act in Christ's name. *For all that are led by the Spirit of God, the same are sons of God* (Rom. 8:14). And only sons can say, *Our Father.*

Our Lord said of Saul of Tarsus: *he is a chosen vessel unto me, to bear my name before the Gentiles and kings and the sons of Israel* (Acts 9:15). Not to them, but before them. So Paul says: *it pleased God, … to reveal his Son in me.* We cannot pray in Christ's name unless we bear that name before people. And this is only possible as long as we *abide in* Him and His words abide in us. So we come to this – unless the heart is right, the prayer must be wrong.

Christ said, *If ye abide in me and my words abide in you, ye shall ask what ye will, and it shall be done unto you* (John 15:7).

Those three promises are really identical; they express the same thought in different words. Look at them:

> *Ask anything in My name, and I will do it* (John 14:13-14).

> *Ask what ye will (if ye abide in me and my words abide in you), and it shall be done* (John 15:7).

> *Ask anything, according to His will, and we have the petitions* (1 John 5:14-15).

And we could sum them all up in the words of John: *and whatsoever we ask, we receive of him because we keep his commandments and do those things that are pleasing in his sight* (1 John 3:22). When we do what He bids, He does what we ask. Listen to God and God will listen to you. Thus, our Lord gives us "power of attorney" over His kingdom, the kingdom of heaven, if only we fulfill the condition of abiding in Him.

Oh, what a wonder this is! How eagerly and earnestly we should seek to know His mind, His wish, His will. How amazing it is that any one of us should, by our own self-seeking, miss such unsearchable riches. We know that God's will is the best for us. We know that He longs to bless us and make us a blessing. We know that to follow our own inclination is absolutely certain to harm us and to hurt us and those whom we love. We know that to turn away from His will for us is to court disaster. O child of God, why do we not trust Him fully and wholly? Here we are, then, once again brought face to face with a life of holiness. We see with the utmost clearness that our Savior's call to prayer is simply a clarion call to holiness. *Be ye holy*, for without holiness no man can see God, and prayer cannot be efficacious.

O child of God, why do we not trust Him fully and wholly?

When we confess that we "never get answers to our prayers," we are not condemning God, or His promises, or the power of prayer, but ourselves. There is no greater test of spirituality than prayer. The man who tries to pray quickly discovers just where he stands in God's sight. Unless we are living the victorious life, we cannot truly pray *in the name* of Christ, and our prayer life must of necessity be feeble, fitful, and often unfruitful.

And *in His name* must be "according to His will." But can we know His will? Assuredly, we can. The apostle Paul not only says, *Let this mind be in you, which was also in Christ Jesus* (Phil. 2:5); he also boldly declares, *we have the mind of Christ* (1 Cor. 2:16 KJV). How, then, can we get to know God's will?

We shall remember that *the secret of the LORD is for those that fear him* (Psalm 25:14).

In the first place, we must not expect God to reveal His will to us unless we desire to know that will and intend to do that will. Knowledge of God's will and the perfor-

Pray we must; pray we can.

mance of that will go together. We are apt to desire to know God's will so we may decide whether we will obey or not. Such

an attitude is disastrous. *If anyone desires to do his will, he shall know of the doctrine* (John 7:17).

God's will is revealed in His Word in the Holy Scriptures. What He promises in His Word I may know to be according to His will.

For example, I may confidently ask for wisdom, because His Word says, *If any of you lacks wisdom, let them ask of God, … and it shall be given them* (James 1:5). We cannot be people of prevailing prayer unless we study God's Word to find out His will for us.

But it is the Holy Spirit of God who is prayer's great Helper. Read again those wonderful words of Paul: *And likewise also the Spirit helps our weakness; for we know not how to pray as we ought, but the Spirit itself makes entreaty for us with groanings which cannot be uttered. But he that searches the hearts knows what is the desire of the Spirit, that according to the will of God, he makes entreaty for the saints* (Rom. 8:26-27).

What comforting words. Ignorance and helplessness in prayer are indeed blessed things if they cast us upon the

Holy Spirit. Blessed be the name of the Lord Jesus. We are left without excuse. Pray we must; pray we can.

Remember, our heavenly Father is pledged to give the Holy Spirit to them that ask Him (Luke 11:13) and any other good thing too (Matt. 7:11).

Child of God, you have often prayed. You have, no doubt, often bewailed your feebleness and slackness in prayer. But have you really prayed in His name?

It is when we have failed and know not what prayers to offer or in what way that the Holy Spirit is promised as our Helper.

Is it not worthwhile to be wholly and wholeheartedly yielded to Christ? The half Christian is of very little use either to God or man. God cannot use him, and man has no use for him, but considers him a hypocrite. One sin allowed in our life wrecks our usefulness and our joy, and robs prayer of its power.

Beloved, we have caught a fresh glimpse of the grace and the glory of our Lord Jesus Christ. He is willing and waiting to share with us both His glory and His grace. He is willing to make us channels of blessing. Shall we not worship God in sincerity and truth, and cry eagerly and earnestly, *What shall I do, Lord?* (Acts 22:10) and then, in the power of His might, do it?

Paul once shot up that prayer to heaven: *What shall I do?* What answer did he get? Listen! He tells us in his counsel to believers everywhere just what it meant to him and should mean to us: *Clothed, therefore, ... with bowels of mercies, with kindness, with humility, with meekness, with tolerance, ... And above all these things put on charity, ... And let the peace of God rule in your hearts, ... Let the word*

*of the Christ dwell in you in abundance in all wisdom, ...
And whatever ye do whether in word or deed, do all in the
name of the Lord Jesus, giving thanks to the God and Father
by him* (Col. 3:12, 14-17).

> *It is only when whatever we do is done in His
> name that He will do whatever we ask in His
> name.*

CHAPTER 7

MUST I AGONIZE?

Prayer is measured, not by time, but by intensity. Earnest souls who read of men like Praying Hyde are today anxiously asking, "Am I expected to pray like that?" They hear of others who sometimes remain on their knees before God all day or all night, refusing food and scorning sleep, while they pray and pray and pray. People naturally wonder, "Are we to do the same? Must all of us follow their examples?" We must remember that those men of prayer did not pray by time. They continued that long in prayer because they could not stop praying.

Some have ventured to think that by what I have said in earlier chapters I have hinted that we must all follow in their manner. Child of God, do not let any such thought – such fear? – distress you. Just be willing to do what He will have you do, what He leads you to do. Think about it; pray about it. We are bidden by the Lord Jesus to pray to our loving heavenly Father. We sometimes sing, "Oh, how He loves." And nothing can fathom that love.

Prayer is not given us as a burden to be borne or an irksome duty to fulfill, but as a joy and power to which there is no limit. It is given us that we may *find grace to help in time of need* (Heb. 4:16). And every time is a *time of need. Pray ye* is an invitation to be accepted rather than a command to be obeyed. Is it a burden for a child to come to his father to ask for some blessing? How a father loves his child and seeks the child's highest good. How he shields that little one from any sorrow or pain or suffering. Our heavenly Father loves us infinitely more than any earthly father. The Lord Jesus loves us infinitely more than any earthly friend. God forgive me if any words of mine on such a precious theme as prayer have wounded the hearts or consciences of those who are yearning to know more about prayer. *Your heavenly Father knoweth*, said our Lord; and if He knows, we can but trust and not be afraid.

A schoolmaster may blame a boy for neglected homework, or tardiness, or frequent absence; but the loving father in the home knows all about it. He knows all about the devoted service of the little child in the home circle, where sickness or poverty throws so many loving tasks in his way. Our dear, loving Father knows all about us. He sees. He knows how little leisure some of us have for prolonged periods of prayer.

For some of us God makes leisure. He makes us lie down (Psalm 23:2) that He may make us look up. Even then, weakness of body often prevents prolonged prayer. Yet I question if any of us, however great and reasonable our excuses, spend enough thought over our prayers. Some of us are bound to be much in prayer. Our very work demands it. We may be looked upon as spiritual leaders; we may be responsible for the spiritual welfare or training of others. God forbid that we should sin against the Lord in ceasing to pray enough for them (1 Sam. 12:23). Yes, with some it is our very business – almost our life's work to pray. Others have friends who give them pain, yet have not sought a friend in Him.

For them they cannot help praying. If we have the burden of souls upon us, we shall never ask, "How long need I pray?"

But how well we know the difficulties which surround the prayer life of many. A little pile of letters lies before me as I write. They are full of excuses and protests and reasonings; it is true. But is that why they are written? No. No. Far from it. In every one of them, there is an undercurrent of deep yearning to know God's will and how to obey the call to prayer amid all the countless claims of life.

If we have the burden of souls upon us, we shall never ask, "How long need I pray?"

Those letters tell of many who cannot get away from others for times of secret prayer, of those who even share bedrooms. They tell of busy mothers, maids, and mistresses who scarcely know how to get through the endless washing and cooking, mending and cleaning, shopping and visiting. They tell of tired workers who are too weary to pray when the day's work is done.

Child of God, our heavenly Father knows all about it. He is not a taskmaster. He is our Father. If you have no time for prayer or no chance of secret prayer, why, just tell Him all about it, and you will discover that you are praying.

To those who seem unable to get any solitude at all or even the opportunity of stealing into a quiet church for a few moments, may we point to the wonderful prayer life of the apostle Paul? Did it ever occur to you that he was in prison when he wrote most of those marvelous prayers of his, which we possess? Picture him. He was chained to a Roman soldier day and night and was never alone for a moment. Epaphras was there part of the time and caught something of his master's passion for prayer. Luke may have been there. What prayer meetings! No opportunity for secret prayer. No, but how much we owe to the uplifting of those chained hands. You and I may never, or rarely ever, be alone, but at least our hands are not fettered with chains, and our hearts are not fettered, nor our lips.

Can we make time for prayer? I may be wrong, but my own belief is that it is not God's will for most of us, and perhaps not for any of us, to spend so much time in prayer as to injure our physical health through getting insufficient food or sleep. With many, it is a physical impossibility, because of bodily weakness, to remain in the spirit of intense prayer for a long time.

The posture in which we pray is immaterial. God will listen whether we kneel, or stand, or sit, or walk, or work.

I am quite aware that many have testified to the fact that God sometimes gives special strength to those who reduce their hours of rest in order to pray more. At one time, I tried getting up very early in the morning, every morning, for prayer and communion with God. After a time, I found that my daily work was suffering in intensity and effectiveness, and it was difficult to keep awake during the early evening hours. But do we pray as much as we might? I do regret that I allowed the days of youth and vigor to pass by without stressing those early hours of prayer.

Now, the inspired command is clear enough: *Pray without ceasing* (1 Thess. 5:17). Our dear Lord said, *it behooves us always to pray and not faint* (Luke 18:1).

This, of course, cannot mean that we are to always be on our knees. I am convinced that God does not wish us to neglect rightful work in order to pray. But it is equally certain that we might work better and do more work, if we gave less time to work and more to prayer.

Let us work well. We are to be *not slothful in business* (Rom. 12:11 KJV). Paul says, *we beseech you, brethren, that ye continue to grow and that ye ... do your business and to work with your hands, ... that ye may walk honestly ... and that ye may desire nothing from any one* (1 Thess. 4:10-12). *If anyone desires not to work neither should he eat* (2 Thess. 3:10).

But are there not endless opportunities during every day of *lifting up holy hands* or at least holy hearts in prayer to our Father? Do we seize the opportunity, as we open our eyes upon each new day of praising and blessing our Redeemer? Every day is an Easter day to the Christian. We can pray as we dress. Without a reminder, we shall often forget. Attach a piece of paper in the corner of your mirror, bearing the words, *Pray without ceasing.* Try it. We can pray as we go from one duty to another. We can often pray at our work. The washing and the writing, the mending and the minding, the cooking and the cleaning will be done all the better for it.

Don't children, both young and old, work better and play better when some loved one is watching? Won't it help us to remember that the Lord Jesus is always with us, watching? Yes, and helping. The very consciousness of His eye upon us will be the consciousness of His power within us.

Do you not think that Paul had this habitual praying in his mind rather than fixed seasons of prayer when he said, *The Lord is near. Be anxious for nothing, but in every thing by prayer and supplication with thanksgiving, let your requests be made known unto God* (Phil. 4:5-6)? Doesn't *in every thing* suggest that, as thing after thing befalls us, moment by moment, we should then and there make it a "thing" of prayer and praise to the Lord Who is near? Why should we limit this "nearness" to the second coming?

What a blessed thought: Prayer is to be near God. When our Lord sent His disciples forth to work, He said, *Behold, I am with you always.*

Sir Thomas Browne, the celebrated physician, had caught this spirit. He made a vow:

> to pray in all places where quietness invites, in any house, highway or street; and to know no street in this city that may not witness that I have not forgotten God and my Savior in it; and that no town or parish where I have been may not say the like. To take occasion of praying upon the sight of any church which I see as I ride about. To pray daily and particularly for my sick patients, and for all sick people, under whose care in any way. And at the entrance into the house of the sick to say, 'The peace and the mercy of God be upon this house.' After a sermon to make a prayer and desire a blessing, and to pray for the minister.

But we question if this habitual communion with our blessed Lord is possible unless we have times, whether long or brief, of definite prayer. And what of these prayer seasons? We have said earlier that prayer is as simple as a little child asking something of his father. Nor would such a remark need any further comment were it not for the existence of the Evil One.

There is no doubt whatever that the Devil opposes our approach to God in prayer and does all he can to prevent the prayer of faith. His chief way of hindering us is to try to fill our minds with the thought of our needs, so they shall not be occupied with thoughts of God, our loving Father, to Whom we pray. He wants us to think more of the gift than of the Giver. The Holy Spirit leads us to pray for a brother. We get as far as "O God, bless my brother," and away go our thoughts to the brother, and his affairs, and his difficulties, his hopes and his fears, and away goes prayer.

How hard the Devil makes it for us to concentrate our thoughts upon God. This is why we urge people to get a realization of the glory of God, and the power of God, and the presence of God, before offering up any petition. If there were no Devil, there would be no difficulty in prayer, but it is the Evil One's chief aim to make prayer impossible. That is why most of us find it hard to sympathize with those who profess to condemn what they call "vain repetitions" and "much speaking" in prayer, quoting our Lord's words in His Sermon on the Mount.

A prominent London vicar said quite recently, "God does not wish us to waste either His time or ours with long prayers. We must be business-like in our dealings with God and just tell Him plainly and briefly what we want and leave the matter there." But does our friend think that prayer is merely making God acquainted with our needs? If that is all there is in it, why, there is no need of prayer. *For your Father knows what things ye have need of before ye ask him,* said our Lord when urging the disciples to pray.

We are aware that Christ Himself condemned some *long prayers* (Matt. 23:14). But they were long prayers made *for a pretext [for a show]* (Luke 20:47). Dear praying people, believe me, the Lord would equally condemn many of the long prayers made every week in some of our prayer meetings – prayers which kill the prayer meeting and finish up with a plea that God would hear these "feeble breathings" or "unworthy utterings."

But He never condemns long prayers that are sincere. Let us not forget that our Lord sometimes spent long nights in prayer. We are told of one of these; we do *He never condemns long prayers that are sincere.* not know how frequently they were (Luke 6:12). Sometimes, *rising up a great while before day*, He would depart to a solitary place for prayer (Mark 1:35). The perfect Man spent more time in prayer than we do. It would seem an undoubted fact that with God's saints in all ages, nights of prayer with God have been followed by days of power with men.

Nor did our Lord excuse Himself from prayer as we, in our ignorance, might think He could have done because of the pressing calls to service and boundless opportunities of usefulness. After one of His busiest days, at a time when His popularity was at its highest, just when everyone sought His company and His counsel, He turned His back upon them all and retired to a mountain to pray (Matt. 14:23).

We are told that once *great multitudes came together to hear and to be healed by him of their infirmities*. Then comes the remark, *But he withdrew himself into the wilderness and prayed* (Luke 5:15-16). Why? Because He knew that prayer was far more potent than service.

We say we are too busy to pray. But the busier our Lord

was, the more He prayed. Sometimes He had no leisure to even eat (Mark 3:20); and sometimes He had no leisure for needed rest and sleep (Mark 6:31). Yet He always took time to pray. If frequent prayer and, at times, long hours of prayer were necessary for our Savior, are they less necessary for us?

I do not write to persuade people to agree with me; that is a very small matter. We only want to know the truth. Spurgeon once said:

There is no need for us to go beating about the bush and not telling the Lord distinctly what it is that we crave at His hands. Nor will it be seemly for us to make any attempt to use fine language; but let us ask God in the simplest and most direct manner for just the things we want ... I believe in business prayers. I mean prayers in which you take to God one of the many promises which He has given us in His Word and expect it to be fulfilled as certainly as we look for the money to be given to us when we go to the bank to cash a check. We should not think of going there, lolling over the counter, chattering with the clerks on every conceivable subject except the one thing for which we had gone to the bank, and then coming away without the coin we needed. But we should lay before the clerk the promise to pay the bearer a certain sum, tell him in what form we wished to take the amount, count the cash after him, and then go on our way to attend to other business. That is just an illustration of the method in which we should draw supplies from the bank of heaven.

Splendid.

But, by all means let us be definite in prayer; by all means let us put eloquence aside if we have any. By all means let us avoid needless "chatter" and come in faith, expecting to receive.

But would the bank clerk pass me the money over the counter so readily if there stood by my side a powerful, evil-countenanced, well-armed ruffian whom he recognized to be a desperate criminal waiting to snatch the money before my weak hands could grasp it? Would he not wait till the ruffian had gone? This is no fanciful picture. The Bible teaches us that, in some way or other, Satan can hinder our prayers and delay the answer. Doesn't Peter urge certain things upon Christians, that their *prayers not be hindered* (1 Peter 3:7)? Our prayers can be hindered. *Then the wicked one comes and catches away that which was sown in his heart* (Matt. 13:19).

Scripture gives us one instance, probably only one out of many, where the Evil One actually kept back – delayed – an answer to prayer for three weeks. We only mention this to show the need of repeated prayer, persistence in prayer, and also to call attention to the extraordinary power which Satan possesses. We refer to Daniel 10:12-13: *Fear not, Daniel: for from the first day that thou didst give thy heart to understand and to afflict thy soul before thy God, thy words were heard, and I am come because of thy words. But the prince of the kingdom of Persia withstood me twenty-one days: and behold, Michael, one of the chief princes, came to help me.*

We must not overlook this satanic opposition and hindrance to our prayers. If we were to be content to ask God only once for some promised thing or one thing we deemed necessary, these chapters would never have been written. Are we never to ask again? For instance, I know that God does not will the death of a sinner. So I come boldly in prayer: "O God, save my friend." Am I never to ask for his conversion again? George Müller prayed daily and more often for sixty years for the conversion of a friend. But what light does the Bible throw upon "business-like" prayers? Our Lord gave two parables to teach persistence and continuance in prayer. The man who asked three loaves from his friend at midnight received as many as he needed *because of his importunity* or persistency, that is, his "shamelessness," as the word literally means (Luke 11:8). The widow who *troubled* the unjust judge with her *continual coming* at last secured redress. Our Lord adds, *And shall not God avenge his own elect who cry day and night unto him though he bears long regarding them?* (Luke 18:7)

How delighted our Lord was with the poor Syrophenician woman who would not take refusals or rebuffs for an answer. Because of her continual request, He said, *O woman, great is thy faith; be it unto thee even as thou desire* (Matt. 15:28). Our dear Lord, in His agony in Gethsemane, found it necessary to repeat even His prayer. *And leaving them, he went away again and prayed the third time, saying the same words* (Matt. 26:44). And we find Paul, the apostle of prayer, asking God time after time to remove his thorn in the flesh. Concerning this thing, says he, *I besought the Lord three times that it might be taken from me* (2 Cor. 12:8).

God cannot always grant our petitions immediately. Sometimes we are not ready to receive the gift. Sometimes He says "No" in order to give us something far better. Think too of the days when Peter was in prison. If your boy was unjustly imprisoned, expecting death at any moment, would you, could you, be content to pray just once, a "business-like" prayer: "O God, deliver my boy from the hands of these men"? Would you not be very much in prayer and very much in earnest?

This is how the church prayed for Peter. *Long and fervent prayer was offered to God by the Church on his behalf* (Acts 12:5 Weymouth). Bible students will have noticed that the King James Version rendering *prayer ... without ceasing* reads *earnest prayer* in the Revised Standard Version. Dr. R. A. Torrey points out that neither translation gives the full

Shall there be no travailing for souls with us?

force of the Greek. The word means literally "stretched out earnestly." It represents the soul stretched by earnest and intense desire. Intense prayer was made for Peter. The very same word is used of our Lord in Gethsemane: *And being in agony, he prayed more earnestly; and his sweat was as it were great drops of blood falling down to the ground* (Luke 22:44).

Ah, there was earnestness, even agony in prayer. Now, what about our prayers? Are we called upon to agonize in prayer? Many of God's dear saints say "No." They think such agonizing in us would reveal great want of faith; yet most of the experiences which befell our Lord are to be ours. We have been crucified with Christ, and we are risen with Him. Shall there be no travailing for souls with us?

Come back to human experience. Can we refrain from agonizing in prayer over dearly beloved children who are living in sin? I question if any believer can have the burden for souls upon him, a passion for souls, and not agonize in prayer.

Can we help crying out like John Knox, "O God, give me Scotland or I die!" Here again the Bible helps us. Wasn't there travail of soul and agonizing prayer when Moses cried out to God, *I pray thee, for, this people who have sinned a great sin and have made themselves gods of gold, that thou wilt forgive their sin; and if not, blot me now out of thy book* (Ex. 32:31-32)?

Was there no agonizing in prayer when Paul said, *I could wish [pray, Weymouth] that myself were anathema from Christ for my brethren* (Rom. 9:3)?

We may, at all events, be quite sure that our Lord, Who wept over Jerusalem, and Who *offered up prayers and supplications with strong crying and tears*, will not be grieved if He sees us weeping over erring ones (Heb. 5:7). Nay, will it not rather gladden His heart to see us agonizing over the sin which grieves Him? In fact, won't the scarcity of conversions in so many ministries be due to lack of agonizing in prayer?

We are told *that Zion travailed, and shall bring forth her sons together* (Isa. 66:8). Was Paul thinking of this passage when he wrote to the Galatians, *My little children, of whom I travail in birth again until Christ is formed in you* (Gal. 4:19)? And will not this be true of spiritual children? Oh, how cold our hearts often are. How little we grieve over the lost. And shall we dare to criticize those who agonize over the perishing? God forbid. No, there is such a thing as wrestling in prayer. Not because God is unwilling to answer, but because of the opposition of the *rulers of this darkness* (Eph. 6:12).

The very word used for *striving* in prayer means "a contest." The contest is not between God and us. He is at one with us in our desires. The contest is with the Evil One, although he is a conquered foe (1 John 3:8). He desires to thwart our prayers.

For we wrestle not against flesh and blood, but against principalities, against powers, against the lords of this age, rulers of this darkness, against the spiritual wickedness in the heavens (Eph. 6:12). We too are in these *heavenly places in Christ* (Eph. 1:3 KJV); and it is only in Christ that we can be victorious. Our wrestling may be a wrestling of our thoughts from thinking Satan's suggestions and keeping them fixed on Christ our Savior – that is, watching as well as praying, *watching in this with all perseverance and supplication* (Eph. 6:18).

We are comforted by the fact that *the Spirit helps our weakness; for we know not how to pray as we ought* (Rom. 8:26). How does the Spirit help us, teach us, if not by example as well as by order? How does the Spirit pray? *The Spirit itself makes entreaty for us with groanings which cannot be uttered* (Rom. 8:26). Does the Spirit agonize in prayer as the Son did in Gethsemane?

If the Spirit prays in us, shall we not share His groanings in prayer? And if our agonizing in prayer weakens our body at the time, will angels come to strengthen us, as they did our Lord (Luke 22:43)? Like Nehemiah, we may weep, and mourn, and fast when we pray before God (Neh. 1:4). "But," one asks, "won't a godly sorrow for sin and a yearning desire for the salvation of others induce in us an agonizing which is unnecessary and dishonoring to God?"

May it not reveal a lack of faith in God's promises? Perhaps it may. But there is little doubt that Paul regarded prayer at least sometimes as a conflict (Rom. 15:30). In writing to the Colossian Christians, he says, *For I would that ye knew what great conflict I have for you ... and for as many as have not seen my face in the flesh, that their hearts might be comforted* (Col. 2:1-2). Undoubtedly, he refers to his prayers for them.

Again, he speaks of Epaphras as one who is *always labouring fervently for you in prayers, that ye may stand firm, perfect and fulfilled in all the will of God* (Col. 4:12).

The word for "strive" is our word *agonize*, the very word used of our Lord being *in agony* when praying Himself (Luke 22:44).

The apostle says again, Epaphras *has a great zeal for you*, that is, in his prayers. Paul saw him praying there in prison and witnessed his intense striving as he engaged in a long, indefatigable effort on behalf of the Colossians. How the praetorian guard to whom Paul was chained must have wondered – yes, and have been deeply touched to see these men at their prayers. Their agitation, their tears, their earnest supplications as they lifted up chained hands in prayer must have been a revelation to him. What would they think of our prayers?

No doubt Paul was speaking of his own custom when he urged the Ephesian Christians and others *to stand firm, ... praying always with all prayer and supplication in the Spirit and watching in this with all perseverance and supplication for all the saints and for me, ... an ambassador in chains* (Eph. 6:11, 18-20). That is a picture of his own prayer life, we may be sure.

So then, prayer meets with obstacles, which must be prayed away. That is what men mean when they talk about praying "through." We must wrestle with the machinations of Satan. It may be bodily weariness or pain, or the insistent claims of other thoughts, or doubt, or the direct assaults of spiritual hosts of wickedness. With us, as with Paul, prayer is something of a *conflict*, a *wrestling*, at least sometimes, which compels us to stir ourselves up *to take hold of thee* (Isa. 64:7). Would we be wrong if we ventured to suggest that very few people ever wrestle in prayer? Do we? But let us never doubt our Lord's power and the riches of His grace.

The author of *The Christian's Secret of a Happy Life* told a little circle of friends, just before her death, of an incident in her own life. Perhaps I may be allowed to tell it abroad. A lady friend who occasionally paid her a visit for two or three days was always a great trial, a veritable tax upon her temper and her patience. Every such visit demanded much prayer preparation. The time came when this "critical Christian" planned a visit for a whole week. She felt that nothing but a whole night of prayer could fortify her for this great testing.

So, providing herself with a little plate of biscuits, she retired in good time to her bedroom to spend the night on her knees before God, to beseech Him to give her grace to keep sweet and loving during the impending visit. No sooner had she knelt beside her bed than there flashed into her mind the words of Philippians 4:19: *But my God shall supply all your need according to his riches in glory by Christ Jesus.*

Her fears vanished. She said, "When I realized that, I gave Him thanks and praised Him for His goodness. Then I jumped into bed and slept the night through. My guest arrived the next day, and I quite enjoyed her visit."

No one can lay down hard-and-fast rules of prayer, even

for himself. God's gracious Holy Spirit alone can direct us moment by moment. That is where, however, we must leave the matter. God is our judge and our guide. But let us remember that prayer is a many-sided thing. As Bishop Dr. H. C. G. Moule says, "True prayer can be uttered under innumerable circumstances." Very often,

> *Prayer is the burden of a sigh*
> *The falling of a tear,*
> *The upward glancing of an eye*
> *When none but God is near.*[11]

It may be just letting your request be made known unto God (Phil. 4:6). We cannot think that prayer need always be a conflict and a wrestle. For if it were, many of us would soon become physical wrecks, suffering from nervous breakdowns, and coming to an early grave.

And with many, it is a physical impossibility to stay any length of time in a posture of prayer. Dr. Moule says, "Prayer, genuine and victorious, is continually offered without the least physical effort or disturbance. It is often in the deepest stillness of soul and body that it wins its longest way. But there is another side of the matter. Prayer is never meant to be indolently easy, however simple and reliant it may be. It is meant to be an infinitely important transaction between man and God. And therefore, very often … it has to be viewed as a work involving labor, persistence, conflict, if it would be prayer indeed."

It is meant to be an infinitely important transaction between man and God.

No one can prescribe for another. Let each be persuaded

---

11   James Montgomery

in his own mind how to pray, and the Holy Spirit will inspire us and guide us in how long to pray. And let us all be so full of the love of God our Savior that prayer, at all times and in all places, may be a joy as well as a means of grace.

> *Shepherd Divine, our wants relieve*
> *In this and every day;*
> *To all Thy tempted followers give*
> *The power to watch and pray.*
>
> *The spirit of interceding grace*
> *Give us the faith to claim;*
> *To wrestle till we see Thy face*
> *And know Thy hidden Name.*

CHAPTER 8

DOES GOD ALWAYS ANSWER PRAYER?

W e now come to one of the most important questions that any man can ask. Much depends upon the answer we are led to give. Let us not shrink from facing the question fairly and honestly. Does God always answer prayer? Of course, we all grant that He does answer prayer – some prayers and sometimes. But does He always answer true prayer? Some so-called prayers He does not answer, because He does not hear them. When His people were rebellious, He said, *when ye make many prayers, I will not hear* (Isa. 1:15).

But a child of God ought to expect answers to prayer. God means every prayer to have an answer; and not a single real prayer can fail in heaven.

And yet that wonderful declaration of Paul, *For all things are yours; ... and ye are Christ's* (1 Cor. 3:21, 23), seems so plainly and so tragically untrue for most Christians. Yet it is not so. They are ours, but many of us do not possess our possessions. The owners of Mount Morgan in Queensland toiled arduously for years on its barren slopes, eking out a miserable existence, never knowing that under their feet was one of the richest sources of gold the world has ever known. There was wealth, vast, undreamt of, yet unimagined and unrealized. It was "theirs," yet not theirs.

The Christian, however, knows of the riches of God in glory in Christ Jesus, but he does not seem to know how to get them. Our Lord tells us that they are to be had for the asking. May He indeed give us all a right judgment in "prayer things." When we say that no true prayer goes unanswered, we are not claiming that God always gives just what we ask for. We do not give our child a red-hot poker because he clamors for it. Have you ever met a parent so foolish as to treat his child like that? Wealthy people are the most careful not to allow their children much pocket money.

Why, if God gave us all we prayed for, we would rule the world, and not Him. And surely we would all confess that we are not capable of doing that. Moreover, more than one ruler of the world is an absolute impossibility.

God's answer to prayer may be "Yes," or it may be "No." It may be "Wait," for it may be that He plans a much larger blessing than we imagined and one which involves other lives as well as our own.

God's answer is sometimes "No." But this is not necessarily a proof of known and willful sin in the life of the petitioner, although there may be sins of ignorance. He said "No" to Paul (2 Cor. 12:8-9). More often than not, the refusal is due to our ignorance or selfishness in asking. *For we know not how to pray as we ought* (Rom. 8:26). That was what was wrong with the mother of Zebedee's children. She came and worshipped our Lord and prayed to Him. He quickly replied, *Ye know not what ye ask* (Matt. 20:22).

Elijah, a great man of prayer, sometimes had "No" for an answer. But when he was swept up to glory in a chariot of fire, did he regret that God said "No" when he cried out, *O LORD, take away my life*?

God's answer is sometimes "Wait." He may delay the answer because we are not yet fit to receive the gift we crave – as with wrestling Jacob. Do you remember the famous prayer of Augustine: "O God, make me pure, but not now"? Are *God's delays are not denials.* not our prayers sometimes like that? Are we always really willing to "drink the cup," to pay the price of answered prayer? Sometimes He delays so that greater glory may be brought to Himself.

God's delays are not denials. We do not know why He sometimes delays the answer and at other times answers before we call (Isa. 65:24). George Müller, one of the greatest men of prayer of all time, had to pray over a period of more than sixty-three years for the conversion of a friend. Who can tell why? "The great point is never to give up until the answer comes," said Müller. "I have been praying for sixty-three years and eight months for one man's conversion. He is not converted yet, but he will be. How can it be otherwise? There is the unchanging promise of Jehovah, and on that I rest." Was this delay due to some persistent hindrance from the Devil? (Dan. 10:13). Was it a mighty and prolonged effort on the part of Satan to shake or break Müller's faith? For no sooner was Müller dead than his friend was converted – even before the funeral.

Yes, his prayer was granted, though the answer was delayed a long time. So many of George Müller's petitions were granted him that it is no wonder that he once exclaimed, "Oh, how good, kind, gracious, and condescending is the One with Whom we have to do. I am only a poor, frail, sinful man, but He has heard my prayers ten thousands of times."

Perhaps some are asking, "How can I discover whether God's answer is 'No' or 'Wait'? How long should I pray if it seems I'm getting no answer?" I believe the Holy Spirit is willing that we know how to pray and will show us whether to continue praying or stop. Even as I write, the postman brings me an illustration. A letter came from one who very rarely writes me, and did not even know my address – one whose name is known to every Christian worker in England. A loved one was stricken down with illness. Is he to continue to pray for her recovery? Is God's answer "No," or is it "Go on praying and wait"? My friend wrote, "I had distinct guidance from God regarding my beloved … that it was the will of God she should be taken … I retired into the rest of surrender and submission to His will. I have much to praise God for." A few hours later God took that loved one to be with Him in glory.

Again, may we urge our readers to hold on to this truth: True prayer never goes unanswered.

If we only gave more thought to our prayers, we would pray more intelligently. That sounds like an obvious truth, but we say it because some dear Christian people seem to lay their common sense and reason aside before they pray. A little reflection would show that God cannot grant some prayers. During the war, every nation prayed for victory. Yet it is perfectly obvious that all countries could not be victorious. Two men living together might pray, the one for rain and the other for fine weather. God cannot give both at the same time in the same place.

But the truthfulness of God is at stake in this matter of prayer. We have all been reading again those marvelous prayer promises of our Lord and have almost staggered at those promises – the wideness of their scope, the fullness of their intent, the largeness of the one word *whatsoever*. Very well, *for God is true* (Rom. 3:4). He certainly will always be found true.

Do not stop to ask me if God has granted all my prayers. He has not. To have said "Yes" to some of them would have spelled curse instead of blessing. To have answered others was, alas, a spiritual impossibility; I was not worthy of the gifts I sought. The granting of some of them would but have fostered spiritual pride and selfsatisfaction. How plain all these things seem now, in the fuller light of God's Holy Spirit.

As we look back and compare our eager, earnest prayers with our poor, unworthy service and lack of true spirituality, we see how impossible it was for God to grant the very things He longed to impart. It was often like asking God to put the ocean of His love into a thimble. And yet, how God just yearns to bless us with every spiritual blessing. How the dear Savior cries again and again, *how often I desired ... and ye would not!* (Matt. 23:37). The sadness of it all is that we often ask and do not receive because of our unworthiness, and then we complain because God does not answer our prayers. The Lord Jesus declares that God gives the Holy Spirit who teaches us how to pray just as readily as a father gives good gifts to his children. But no gift is a good gift if the child is not fit to use that gift. God never gives us something that we cannot, or will not, use for His glory. (I am not referring to talents, for we may abuse or "bury" those, but to spiritual gifts.)

Did you ever see a father give his baby boy a razor when he asked for it, because he hoped the boy would grow into a man and then find the razor useful? Doesn't a father say to his child, "Wait till you are older, or bigger, or wiser, or better, or stronger"? Won't our loving heavenly Father also say to us, "Wait"? In our ignorance and blindness we must surely sometimes say:

> *In very love refuse*
> *Whate'er Thou seest*
> *Our weakness would abuse.*

Rest assured that God never bestows tomorrow's gift today. It is not unwillingness on His part to give. It is not that God is ever confined by Himself. His resources are infinite, and His ways are past finding out. It was after bidding His disciples to ask, that our Lord goes on to hint not only at His providence, but at His resources. *Behold the fowls of the air, … yet your heavenly Father feeds them* (Matt. 6:26). How simple it sounds. Yet have you ever reflected that not a single millionaire, the wide world over, is wealthy enough to feed all the birds of the air, even for one day? Your heavenly Father feeds them every day and is none the poorer for it. Shall He not much more feed you, clothe you, and take care of you?

Oh, let us rely more upon prayer! Do we not know that *he is a rewarder of those that diligently seek him* (Heb. 11:6)?

The oil of the Holy Spirit will never cease to flow as long as there are empty vessels to receive it (2 Kings 4:6). We are always to blame when the Spirit's work ceases. God cannot trust some Christians with the fullness of the Holy Spirit. God cannot trust some workers with definite spiritual results in their labors. They would suffer from pride and vainglory. No, we do not claim that God grants every Christian everything he prays for.

As we saw in an earlier chapter, we must have purity of heart, purity of motive, and purity of desire, if our prayers are to be in His name. God is greater than His promises and often gives more than we desire or deserve, but He does not always do so. So, if any specific petition is not granted, we may feel sure that God is calling us to examine our hearts. For He has undertaken to grant every prayer that is truly offered in His name.

Let us repeat His blessed words once more; we cannot repeat them too often: *And whatsoever ye shall ask the Father in my name, that will I do, that the Father may be glorified in the Son. If ye ask any thing in my name, I will do it* (John 14:13-14). Remember that it was impossible for Christ to offer up any prayer which was not granted. He was God; He knew the mind of God; He had the mind of the Holy Spirit. Does He once say, *Father, if it be possible, let …* as He kneels in agony in Gethsemane's garden, pouring out strong crying and tears? Yes, and He *was heard because of his reverent fear* (Heb. 5:7). Surely not the agony, but the sonlike fear, gained the answer. Our prayers are heard not because they are urgent but because they are filial.

Fellow Christian, we cannot fully understand that hallowed scene of dreadful awe and wonder. But this we know:

Our Lord never yet made a promise which He cannot keep or does not mean to fulfill. The Holy Spirit makes intercession for us (Rom. 8:26), and God cannot say "Nay" to Him. The Lord Jesus makes intercession for us (Heb. 7:25), and God cannot say "Nay" to Him. His prayers are worth a thousand of ours, but it is He who bids us pray.

"But wasn't Paul filled with the Holy Spirit?" you ask. "And didn't he say, 'We have the mind of Christ'? Yet he asked three times that God would remove the thorn in his flesh, and yet God distinctly told him He would not do so."

It is a remarkable thing that the only petition recorded of Paul seeking something for his own individual need was refused! The difficulty, however, is this: Why did Paul, who had the mind of Christ, ask for something that he soon discovered was contrary to God's wishes? There are doubtless many fully consecrated Christians reading these words who have been perplexed because God has not given some things they prayed for.

We must remember that we may be filled with the Spirit and yet err in judgment or desire. We must remember too that we are never filled with God's Holy Spirit once for all. The Evil One is always on the watch to put his mind into us to strike at God through us. At any moment we may become disobedient or unbelieving, or may be betrayed into some thought or act contrary to the Spirit of love.

We have an astonishing example of this in the life of Peter. At one moment, under the compelling influence of God's Holy Spirit, he cries, *Thou art the Christ, the Son of the living God.* Our Lord turns, and with words of high commendation says, *Blessed art thou, Simon son of Jonah, for flesh and blood has not revealed it unto thee, but my*

Father who is in the heavens. Yet, a very little while after, the Devil gets his mind into Peter, and our Lord turns and says unto him, *Remove thyself from before me, Satan* (Matt. 16:16-17, 23). Peter was now speaking in the name of Satan. Satan still desires to have us.

Paul was tempted to think that he could do far better work for his beloved Master if only that "thorn" could be removed. But God knew that Paul would be a better man with the thorn than without it.

Is it not a comfort to us to know that we may bring more glory to God under something which we are apt to regard as a hindrance or handicap, than if that undesired thing was removed? *My grace is sufficient for thee; for my strength is made perfect in weakness* (2 Cor. 12:9). Remember that:

> *God nothing does, nor suffer to be done,*
> *But what thou would'st thyself*
> *Did'st thou but see*
> *The end of all He does as well as He.*

Paul was not infallible; nor was Peter or John; nor is the Pope or any other man. We may, and do, offer up mistaken prayers. The highest form of prayer is not, "Thy way, O God, not mine," but "My way, O God, is Thine." We are taught to pray, not "Thy will be changed," but "Thy will be done."

May we, in conclusion, give the testimony of two who have proved that God can be trusted?

Sir H. M. Stanley, the great explorer, wrote, "I for one must not dare to say that prayers are inefficacious. Where I have been in earnest, I have been answered. When I prayed for light to guide my followers wisely through the perils that beset them, a ray of light has come upon the perplexed mind, and a clear road to deliverance has been pointed out. You may know when prayer is answered by the glow of content, which fills one who has flung his cause before God, as he rises to his feet. I have evidence, satisfactory to myself, that prayers are granted."

Mary Slessor, whose life story in West Africa has surely thrilled us all, was once asked what prayer meant to her. She replied, "My life is one long, daily, hourly record of answered prayer for physical health, for mental over-strain, for guidance given marvelously, for errors and dangers averted, for enmity to the gospel subdued, for food provided at the exact hour needed, for everything that goes to make up life and my poor service. I can testify with a full and often wonder-stricken awe that I believe God answers prayer. I know God answers prayer!"

CHAPTER 9

ANSWERS TO PRAYER

Mere human nature would choose a more startling title to this chapter. Remarkable answers, wonderful answers, amazing answers. But we must allow God to teach us that it is as natural for Him to answer prayer as it is for us to ask. How He delights to hear our petitions, and how He loves to answer them. When we hear of some wealthy person giving a treat to poverty-stricken people or wiping out some crushing deficit in a missionary society, we exclaim, "How nice to be able to do a thing like that." Well, if it is true that God loves us and we know it is true, don't you think it gives Him great joy to give us what we ask? We should like, therefore, to recount one or two answers to prayer out of many, which have come to our notice, so that we may have greater boldness in coming to the throne of grace. God saves men for whom we pray. Try it.

In discussing this question with a man of prayer a few days ago, he suddenly asked me, "Do you know Saint M's Church?"

"Quite well, I've have been there several times."

"Let me tell you what happened when I lived there.

We had a prayer meeting each Sunday before the eight o'clock communion service. As we rose from our knees one Sunday, a sidesman said, 'Vicar, I wish you would pray for my boy. He is twenty-two years old now and has not been to church for years.'"

"We can spare five minutes now," replied the vicar. They knelt down again and offered up earnest supplication on behalf of that man. Although nothing was said to him about this, that youth came to church that same evening. Something in the sermon convicted him of sin. He came into the vestry, brokenhearted, and accepted Jesus Christ as his Savior.

On Monday morning, my friend, who was working as a church army captain in the parish, was present at the weekly meeting of the staff. He said to the vicar, "That conversion last night is a challenge to prayer, a challenge from God. Shall we accept it?"

"What do you mean?" asked the vicar.

"Well," said he, "shall we single out the worst man in the parish and pray for him?" By unanimous consent they fixed upon K as the worst man they knew. So they "agreed" in prayer for his conversion. At the end of that week, as they were conducting a Saturday night prayer meeting in the mission hall and while his very name was on their lips, the door swung open and in staggered K, much the worse for liquor. He had never been in that mission hall before. Without thinking of removing his cap, he sank onto a chair near the door and buried his face in his hands. The prayer meeting suddenly became an enquiry room. Even as he was in drink, he sought the Lord Who was seeking him. Nor did he ever go back. Today he is one of the finest dockyard missionaries in the land.

Oh, why do we not pray for our unconverted friends? They may not listen to us when we plead with them, but they cannot hold out if we pray for them. Let two or three agree in prayer over the salvation of the worst, and then see what God will do. Tell God and then trust God. God works in a wonderful way, as well as in a mysterious way, His wonders to perform.

Dan Crawford told us recently that when returning to his mission field after a furlough, it was necessary to make all possible haste. But a deep stream, which had to be crossed, was flooded, and no boats were available, or usable, for that matter. So he and his party camped and *Oh, why do we not pray for our unconverted friends?* prayed. An infidel might well have laughed aloud. How could God get them across that river? But, as they prayed, a tall tree, which had battled with that river for scores of years, began to totter and fall. It fell clear across the stream. As Mr. Crawford says, "The Royal Engineers of heaven had laid a pontoon bridge for God's servants."

Many young people will read these prayer stories. May we remind them that God still hears the voice of the lad and, yes, the lass (Gen. 21:17). For them, may we be allowed to add the following story with the earnest desire that prayer may be their heritage, their very life, and that answered prayer may be their daily experience.

Some little time ago, a Chinese boy of twelve years old, named Ma Na Si, a boarder in the mission school at Chefoo, went home for the holidays. He is the son of a native pastor.

While standing on the doorstep of his father's house,

he saw a horseman galloping towards him. The man, a heathen, was in a great state of perturbation. He eagerly enquired for the "Jesus man," the pastor. The boy told him that his father was away from home. The poor man was distressed and hurriedly explained the reason for his visit. He had been sent from a heathen village some miles away to fetch the "holy man" to cast a devil out of the daughter-in-law of a heathen friend. He poured out his sad story of this young woman, torn by devils, raving and reviling, pulling out her hair, clawing her face, tearing her clothes, smashing up furniture, and dashing away dishes of food. He told of her spirit of sacrilege, outrageous impiety, and brazen blasphemy, and how these outbursts were followed by foaming at the mouth and great exhaustion, both physical and mental. "But my father is not at home," the boy kept reiterating.

At length the frenzied man seemed to understand. Suddenly, he fell on his knees and, stretching out his hands in desperation, cried, "You too are a Jesus man; will you come?"

Think of it: a boy of twelve. Yes, but even a lad, when fully yielded to his Savior, is not fearful of being used by that Savior. There was but one moment of surprise and a moment of hesitation, and then the laddie put himself wholly at his Master's disposal. Like little Samuel of old, he was willing to obey God in all things. He accepted the earnest entreaty as a call from God. The heathen stranger sprang into the saddle, and, swinging the Christian boy up behind him, he galloped away.

Ma Na Si began to think things over. He had accepted an invitation to cast out a devil in the name of Christ Jesus.

But was he worthy to be used of God in this way? Was his heart pure and his faith strong? As they galloped along, he carefully searched his own heart for sin to be confessed and repented of. He prayed for guidance concerning what to say and how to act; he tried to recall Bible instances of demoniacal possession and how they were dealt with. Then he simply and humbly cast himself upon the God of power and of mercy, asking His help for the glory of the Lord Jesus.

On arrival at the house, they found that some of the members of the family were forcefully holding down the tortured woman upon the bed. Although she had not been told that a messenger had gone for the native pastor, as soon as she heard footsteps in the court outside, she cried, "All of you get out of my way quickly, so that I can escape. I must flee. A 'Jesus man' is coming. I cannot endure him. His name is Ma Na Si."

Ma Na Si entered the room and after a ceremonial bow, knelt down, and began to pray. Then he sang a Christian hymn to the praise of the Lord Jesus. Then, in the name of the risen Lord, glorified and omnipotent, he commanded the demon to come out of the woman. At once, she was calm, though prostrate with weakness. From that day on, she was perfectly whole. She was amazed when they told her that she had uttered the name of the Christian boy, for she had never heard of it or read of it before, because that whole village was heathen. But that day was veritably a beginning of days to those people, for from it, the Word of the Lord had free course and was glorified.

Beloved reader, I do not know how this little narrative affects you. It is one that moves me to the very depths of my being. It seems to me that most of us know so little of the power of God, so little of His overwhelming, irresistible love. Oh, what love is His! Now, every time we pray, that wonderful love envelops us in a special way.

If we really loved our blessed Savior, shouldn't we seek communion with Him in prayer more often? Fellow Christian, is it because we pray so little that we criticize so much? Oh, let us remember that we, like our dear Savior, are not sent into the world to condemn, to judge, the world, *but that the world through him might be saved* (John 3:17).

Will any thoughtless word of criticism of anyone move anyone nearer to Christ? Will it even help the utterer of that faultfinding to be more like the Master? Oh, let us lay

Will any thoughtless word of criticism of anyone move anyone nearer to Christ?

aside the spirit of criticism, of blaming, of faultfinding, of disparaging others or their work. Wouldn't Paul say to us all, *And such were some of you, but now ye are washed* (1 Cor. 6:11)?

Do you see what we are aiming at? All the evil dispositions and failings we detect in others are due to the Devil. It is the Evil One in the heart who causes those words and deeds, which we are so ready to condemn and to exaggerate. Demon possession is not unknown in England, but it takes a different form, perhaps. Our very friends and acquaintances, so kind and lovable, are often tied and bound by some besetting sin *whom Satan hath bound* these many years.

We may plead with them in vain. We may warn them in vain. Courtesy and charity and our own failings and shortcomings forbid us standing over them like Ma Na Si and exorcising the evil spirit. But have we tried prayer,

prayer always backed up by love which cannot be provoked (1 Cor. 13:5)?

God answers prayer from old and young, when there is a clean heart, a holy life, and a simple faith. God answers prayer. We are but frail and faulty servants at best. Sincere as we may be, we shall sometimes ask amiss. But God that promised is faithful, and He will guard us from all harm and supply every need.

> *Can I have the things I pray for?*
> *God knows best;*
> *He is wiser than His children.*
> *I can rest.*

Beloved, if our heart does not condemn us, then we have confidence in God; and whatsoever we ask, we receive of him because we keep his commandments and do those things that are pleasing in his sight (1 John 3:21-22).

CHAPTER 10

HOW GOD ANSWERS PRAYER

For man fully to understand God and all His dealings with us is an utter impossibility. *O the depth of the riches both of the wisdom and of the knowledge of God! How incomprehensible are his judgments and his ways past finding out!* (Rom. 11:33). True, but we need not make difficulties where none exist. If God has all power and all knowledge, surely prayer has no difficulties, though occasionally there may be perplexities. We cannot discover God's method, but we know something of His manner of answering prayer.

But at the very outset may we remind ourselves how little we know about ordinary things? Mr. Thomas Edison, whose knowledge is profound, wrote in August 1921, "We don't know the millionth part of one percent about anything. We don't know what water is. We don't know what light is. We don't know what gravitation is. We don't know what enables us to keep on our feet to stand up. We don't know what electricity is. We don't know what heat is. We don't know anything about magnetism. We have a lot of hypotheses, but that is all." But we do not allow our ignorance about all these things to deprive us of their use. We do not know much about prayer, but surely this need not prevent us from praying. We do know what our Lord has taught us about prayer. And we do know that He has sent the Holy Spirit to teach us all things (John 14:26).

How, then, does God answer prayer? One way is just this: He reveals His mind to those who pray. His Holy Spirit puts fresh ideas into the minds of praying people. We are quite aware that the Devil and his angels are busy enough putting bad thoughts into our minds. Surely, then, God and His holy angels can give us good thoughts. Even poor, weak, sinful men and women can put good thoughts into the minds of others. That is what we try to do in writing. We do not stop to think what a wonderful thing it is that a few peculiarly shaped black marks on this white paper can uplift and inspire, or depress and cast down, or even convict of sin. But, to an untutored savage, it is a stupendous miracle. Moreover, you and I can often read people's thoughts or wishes from an expression on the face or a glance of the eye. Even though transference between one person and another is commonplace today, God can convey His thoughts to us in many ways. A remarkable instance of this was related by a speaker last year at Northfield. Three or four years ago, he met an old whaling captain who told him this story.

"A good many years ago, I was sailing in the desolate seas off Cape Horn, hunting whales. One day we were beating directly south in the face of a hard wind. We had been tacking this way and that all the morning and were making very little headway. About eleven o'clock, as I stood at the wheel, the idea suddenly came into my mind, 'Why batter the ship against these waves? There are probably as many whales to the north as to the south. Suppose we run with the wind instead of against it?' In response to that sudden idea, I changed the course of the ship and sailed north instead of south.

"One hour later, at noon, the lookout at the masthead shouted, 'Boats ahead!' Presently we overtook four lifeboats, in which were fourteen sailors, the only survivors of the crew of a ship, which had burned to the water's edge ten days before. Those men had been adrift in their boats ever since, frantically praying to God for rescue; and we arrived just in time to save them. They could not have survived another day."

Prayer gives God the opportunity of speaking to us and revealing His will to us.

Then the old whaler added, "I don't know whether you believe in religion or not, but I happen to be a Christian. I have begun every day of my life with prayer that God would use me to help someone else, and I am convinced that God, that day, put the idea into my mind to change the course of my ship. That idea was the means of saving fourteen lives."

God has many things to say to us. He has many thoughts to put into our minds. We are apt to be so busy doing His work that we do not stop to listen to His Word. Prayer gives God the opportunity of speaking to us and revealing His will to us. May our attitude often be: *Speak, Lord, for thy slave hears.*

God answers other prayers by putting new thoughts into the minds of those we pray for. At a series of services dealing with the victorious life, one afternoon I urged the congregation to "make up" their quarrels if they really desired a holy life. One lady went straight home, and after very earnest prayer, wrote to her sister, with whom, owing to some disagreement, she had had nothing to do for twenty years. Her sister was living thirty miles away. The very next morning the writer of that note received a letter from that sister asking forgiveness and seeking reconciliation. The two letters had crossed in the mail. While the one sister was praying to God for the other, God was speaking to that other sister, putting into her mind the desire for reconciliation.

You may say, Why didn't God put that desire there before? It may be that He foresaw that it would be useless for the distant sister to write asking forgiveness until the other sister was also willing to forgive. The fact remains that, when we pray for others, somehow or other it opens the way for God to influence those we pray for. God needs our prayers, or He would not beg us to pray.

A little time back, at the end of a weekly prayer meeting, a godly woman begged those present to pray for her husband, who would never go near a place of worship. The leader suggested that they should continue in prayer then and there. Most earnest prayers were offered up. Now, the husband was devoted to his wife, and frequently came to meet her. He did so that night and arrived at the hall while the prayer meeting was still in progress. God put it into his mind to open the door and wait inside, a thing he had never done before. As he sat on a chair near the door, leaning his head upon his hand, he overheard those earnest petitions. During the homeward walk he said, "Wife, who was the man they were praying for tonight?"

"Oh," she replied, "it is the husband of one of our workers."

"Well, I am quite sure he will be saved," said he. "God

must answer prayers like that." A little later in the evening he again asked, "Who was the man they were praying for?"

She replied in similar terms as before. On retiring to rest, he could not sleep. He was under deep conviction of sin. Awaking his wife, he begged her to pray for him.

How clearly this shows us that when we pray, God can work. God could have prompted that man to enter that prayer meeting any week. But had he done so, it is questionable whether any good at all would have come from it. When once those earnest, heart-felt petitions were being offered up on his behalf, God saw that they would have a mighty influence upon that poor man.

It is when we pray that God can help us in our work and strengthen our resolves. For we can answer many of our own prayers. One bitter winter a prosperous farmer was praying that God would keep a neighbor from starving. When the family prayers were over, his little boy said, "Father, I don't think I should have troubled God about that."

"Why not?" his father asked.

"Because it would be easy enough for you to see that they don't starve." There is not the slightest doubt that if we pray for others, we shall also try to help them.

A young convert asked his vicar to give him some Christian work. "Have you a buddy?"

"Yes," replied the boy.

"Is he a Christian?"

"No, he is as careless as I was."

"Then go and ask him to accept Christ as his Savior."

"Oh, no," said the lad, "I could never do that. Give me anything but that."

"Well," said the vicar, "promise me two things: that you

will not speak to him about his soul, and that you will pray to God twice daily for his conversion."

"Why, yes, I'll gladly do that," answered the boy. Before two weeks were up, he rushed round to the vicarage. "Will you let me off my promise? I must speak to my friend!" he cried. When he began to pray, God could give him strength to witness. Communion with God is essential before we can have real communion with our fellow man. My belief is that people seldom speak to others about their spiritual condition because they pray so little for them.

I have never forgotten how my faith in prayer was confirmed when, as a lad of thirteen, I earnestly asked God to enable me on a certain day to secure twenty new subscribers for missions overseas. Exactly twenty new names were secured before night closed in. The consciousness that God would grant that prayer was an incentive and gave an unusual courage in approaching others.

A cleric in England suggested to his people that they should pray each day for the worst man or woman and then go to them and tell them about Jesus. Only six agreed to do so. On arriving home, he began to pray. Then he said, "I must not leave this to my people. I must take it up myself. I don't know the bad people. I'll have to go out and enquire." Approaching a rough-looking man at a street corner, he asked, "Are you the worst man in this district?"

"No, I'm not."

"Would you mind telling me who is?"

"I don't mind. You'll find him at number seven, down that street."

He knocked at number seven and entered. "I'm looking for the worst man in my parish. They tell me it might be you?"

"Whoever told you that? Fetch him here and show him who's the worst man. No, there are lots worse than me."

"Well, who is the worst man you know?"

"Everybody knows him. He lives at the end house in that court. He's the worst man."

So down the court he went and knocked at the door. A surly voice cried, "Come in!" There were a man and his wife.

"I hope you'll excuse me, but I'm the minister of the chapel along the round. I'm looking for the worst man in my district, because I have something to tell him. Are you the worst man?"

The man turned to his wife and said, "Lass, tell him what I said to you five minutes ago."

"No, tell him yourself."

"What were you saying?" enquired the cleric.

"Well, I've been drinking for twelve weeks. I've had the DT's [delirium tremens] and have pawned all in the house worth pawning. And I said to my wife a few minutes ago, 'Lass, this thing has to stop, and if it doesn't, I'll stop it myself. I'll go and drown myself.' Then you knocked at the door. Yes, sir, I'm the very worst man. What have you got to say to me?"

"I'm here to tell you that Jesus Christ is the greatest Savior, and that He can make out of the worst man one of the best. He did it for me, and He will do it for you."

"Do you think He can do it even for me?"

"I'm sure He can. Kneel down and ask Him."

Not only was the poor drunkard saved from his sins,

but he is today also a radiant Christian man, bringing other drunken people to the Lord Jesus Christ.

Surely none of us finds it difficult to believe that God can, in answer to prayer, heal the body, send rain or fair weather, dispel fogs, or avert calamities.

We have a God whose knowledge is infinite. *He knows our frame* for He made it (Psalm 103:14). He knows it far

God must be allowed to work in His own way.

better than the cleverest doctor or surgeon. He made and He can restore. We believe that God allows us to use medical skill, but we also believe that God, by His wonderful

knowledge, can heal, and does heal, without human cooperation. And God must be allowed to work in His own way. We are so apt to tie God down to the way we approve of; God's aim is to glorify His name in answering our prayers. Sometimes He sees that our desire is right, but our petition is wrong. Paul thought he could bring more glory to God if only the thorn in his flesh could be removed. God knew that he would be a better man and do better work with the thorn than without it. So God said, "No, No, and No" to his prayer, and then explained why.

So it was with Monica, who prayed many years for the conversion of Augustine, her licentious son. When he was determined to leave home and cross the seas to Rome, she prayed earnestly, even passionately, that God would keep him by her side and under her influence. She went down to a little chapel on the seashore to spend the night in prayer, close to where the ship lay at anchor. But, when morning came, she found that the ship had sailed even while she prayed. Her petition was refused, but her real desire was granted. For it was in Rome that Augustine met the sainted

Ambrose, who led him to Christ. How comforting it is to know that God knows what is best.

But we should never think it unreasonable that God should make some things dependent upon our prayers. Some people say that if God really loves us, He would give us what is best for us whether we ask Him or not. Dr. Harry Fosdick has so beautifully pointed out that God has left man many things to do for himself. He promises seedtime and harvest. Yet man must prepare the soil, sow, till, and reap in order to allow God to do His share. God provides us with food and drink. But He leaves us to take, and eat, and drink. There are some things God cannot do, or at least will not do, without our help. God cannot do some things unless we think. He never emblazons His truth upon the sky. The laws of science have always been there.

But we must think, and experiment, and think again if we want to use those laws for our own good and God's glory.

God cannot do some things unless we work. He stores marble in the hills, but He has never built a cathedral. He fills the mountains with iron ore, but He never makes a needle or a locomotive. He leaves that to us. We must work.

If, then, God has left many things dependent upon man's thinking and working, why should He not leave some things dependent upon man's praying? He has done so. *Ask and ye shall receive.* And there are some things God will not give us unless we ask. Prayer is one of the three ways in which man can cooperate with God; and the greatest of these is prayer.

Men of power are without exception men of prayer. God bestows His Holy Spirit in His fullness only on men of prayer. And it is through the operation of the Spirit that answers to prayer come. Every believer has the Spirit of Christ dwelling in him. For *if anyone does not have the Spirit of Christ, that person is not of him.* But a man of prevailing prayer must be filled with the Spirit of God.

A lady missionary wrote recently that it had been said of Praying Hyde that he never spoke to an unconverted man but that he was soundly converted. But if he ever did fail at first to touch a heart for God, he went back to his room and wrestled in prayer till he was shown what it was in himself that had hindered his being used by God. Yes, when we are filled with the Spirit of God, we cannot help influencing others Godward. But, to have power with men, we must have power with God.

The momentous question for you and me is not, however, "How does God answer prayer?" The question is, "Do I really pray?" What a marvelous power God places at our disposal. Do we for a moment think that anything displeasing to God is worth holding on to? Fellow Christian, trust Christ wholly, and you will find Him wholly true.

Let us give God the chance to put His mind into us, and we shall never doubt the power of prayer again.

CHAPTER 11

HINDRANCES TO PRAYER

The poet said, and we often sing:

What various hindrances we meet
In coming to the mercy seat.

Yes, indeed, they are various. But here again, most of those hindrances are of our own making.

God wants me to pray. The Devil does not want me to pray and does all he can to hinder me. He knows that we can accomplish more through our prayers than through our work. He would rather have us do anything else than pray.

We have already referred to Satan's opposition to prayer:

Angels our march oppose,
Who still in strength excel,
Our enemy, sworn, relentless, foe,
Countless, invisible.

But we need not fear them, nor heed them, if our eyes are always on the Lord. The holy angels are stronger than fallen angels, and we can leave the celestial hosts to guard us. We believe we owe those wandering thoughts to the hosts of evil, which so often wreck prayer. As soon as we kneel, we remember something that should have been done or something which had better be seen to at once.

These thoughts come from without and are surely due to the promptings of evil spirits. The only cure for wandering thoughts is to get our minds fixed upon God. Undoubtedly, a man's worst foe is himself. Prayer is for a child of God, and one who is living as a child of God should pray.

The great question is: Am I harboring any foes in my heart? Are there traitors within? God cannot give us His best spiritual blessings unless we fulfill conditions of trust, obedience, and service. Don't we often ask earnestly for the highest spiritual gifts without even any thought of fulfilling the necessary requirements? Don't we often ask for blessings we are not fitted to receive? Dare we be honest with ourselves, alone in the presence of God? Dare we say sincerely, *Search me, O God, and know my heart*? Is there anything in me which is hindering God's blessing for me and through me? We discuss the "problem of prayer"; we are the problem that needs discussing or dissecting. Prayer is all right. There is no problem in prayer to the heart, which is absolutely stayed on Christ.

Now, we shall not quote the usual Bible texts, which show how prayer may be frustrated. We merely desire that everyone should get a glimpse of his own heart. No sin is too small to hinder prayer and perhaps to turn the very prayer itself into sin, if we are not willing to renounce that sin. The Muslims in West Africa have a saying: "If there is no purity, there is no prayer; if there is no prayer, there is no drinking of the water of heaven." This truth is so clearly taught in Scripture that it is amazing that any should try to retain both sin and prayer. Yet, many do this. Even David cried, long ages ago, *If I regard iniquity in my heart, the Lord will not hear me* (Psalm 66:18).

And Isaiah says, *But your iniquities have separated between you and your God, and your sins have hid his face from you* (Isa. 59:2). Surely we must all agree that it is sin in us, and not the unwillingness of Christ to hear, that hinders prayer. As a rule, it is some little sin, so-called, that mars and spoils the prayer life. There may be:

(1) Doubt. Now, unbelief is possibly the greatest hindrance to prayer. Our Lord said that the Holy Spirit would convict the world of sin – *of sin, because they do not believe in me* (John 16:9). We are not *of the world*, yet is there not much practical unbelief in many of us? Writing to believers, James says, *But ask in faith, not doubting anything. For he that doubts ... let not such a man think that he shall receive anything of the Lord* (James 1:6-7). Some have not because they ask not. Others have not because they believe not. Did you think it a little strange that we spent so much time on adoration and thanksgiving before we came to the asking? But surely, if we get a glimpse of the glorious majesty of our Lord and the wonders of His love and grace, unbelief and doubt will vanish away as mists before the rising sun. Wasn't this the reason that Abraham *doubted not ... with unbelief,* in that he gave God the glory due unto His name, and was therefore *fully persuaded that he was also powerful to do all* (Rom. 4:20-21)? Knowing

> *Unbelief is possibly the greatest hindrance to prayer.*

what we do of God's stupendous love, is it not amazing that we should ever doubt?

(2) Then there is self – the root of all sin. How selfish we are prone to be even in our good works. How we hesitate to give up anything which "self" craves for. Yet we know that a full hand cannot take Christ's gifts. Was this why the Savior, in the prayer He first taught, coupled us with everything else? *Our* is the first word. *Our Father … give us … forgive us … deliver us ….*

Pride prevents prayer, for prayer is a very humbling thing. How hateful pride must be in the sight of God. God is the One who gives us all things *richly to enjoy. What hast thou that thou didst not receive?* asks Paul (1 Cor. 4:7). Surely, surely, we are not going to let pride, with its hateful, ugly sister, jealousy, ruin our prayer life. God cannot do great things for us whereby we may be glad, if they are going to "turn our heads." Oh, how foolish we can be. Sometimes, when we are insistent, God does give us what we ask, at the expense of our holiness. *And he gave them their request, but sent leanness into their soul* (Psalm 106:15). O God, save us from that – save us from self. Again, self asserts itself in criticizing others. Let this thought burn itself into your memory: the more like Jesus Christ a man becomes, the less he judges other people. It is an infallible test. Those who are always criticizing others have drifted away from Christ. They may still be His, but they have lost His Spirit of love. Beloved reader, if you have a criticizing nature, allow it to dissect yourself and never your neighbor. You will be able to give it full scope, and it will never be unemployed. Is this a harsh remark? Does it betray a tendency to commit the very sin – for it is sin – it condemns? It would if it were spoken to any one individual. But its object is to pierce armor, which is seemingly invulnerable. And no one, who for one month has kept his tongue "from picking and stealing" the reputation of other people, will ever desire to go back again to backbiting. *Charity [Love] suffereth long, and is kind* (1 Cor. 13:4 KJV). Do we? Are we?

We are ourselves no better because we have managed to paint other people in worse colors than ourselves. But, oddly enough, we enhance our own spiritual joy and our own living witness for Christ when we refuse to pass on disparaging information about others, or when we refrain from judging the work or lives of other people. It may be hard at first, but it soon brings untold joy and is rewarded by the love of all. It is most hard to keep silent in the face of "modern" heresies. Are we not told to *earnestly persevere in the faith which was given once unto the saints* (Jude 3)? Sometimes we must speak out, but let it always be in the spirit of love. "Rather let error live than love die."

Even in our private prayers, faultfinding of others must be resolutely avoided. Read once more the story of John Hyde praying for the "cold brother." Believe me, a criticizing spirit destroys holiness of life more easily than anything else, because it is such an eminently respectable sin and makes such easy victims of us. We need scarcely add that when a believer is filled with the Spirit of Christ Who is Love, he will never tell others of the un-Christian behavior he may discern in his friends. "He was most rude to me"; "He is too conceited"; "I can't stand that man"; and such like remarks are surely unkind, unnecessary, and often untrue.

Our dear Lord suffered the contradiction of sinners against Himself, but He never complained or published abroad the news to others. Why should we do so? Self must be dethroned if Christ is to reign supreme. There must be no idols in the heart. Do you remember what God said of some leaders of religion? *These men have caused their uncleanness to come up over their heart ... should I be enquired of at all by them?* (Ezek. 14:3).

When our aim is solely the glory of God, then God can answer our prayers. Christ Himself, rather than His gifts, should be our desire. *Delight thyself in the LORD, and he shall give thee the desires of thy heart* (Psalm 37:4).

> *Beloved, if our heart does not condemn us, then we have confidence in God; and whatsoever we ask, we receive of him because we keep his commandments and do those things that are pleasing in his sight*
> (1 John 3:21-22).

It is as true today as in the early days of Christianity that men ask and receive not, because they ask amiss that they may spend it on their pleasures, that is, self (James 4:3).

(3) Unlove in the heart is possibly the greatest hindrance to prayer. A loving spirit is a condition of believing prayer. We cannot be wrong with man and right with God. The spirit of prayer is essentially the spirit of love. Intercession is simply love at prayer.

> *He prayeth best who loveth best*
> *All things both great and small;*
> *For the great God Who loveth us,*
> *He made and loveth all.*

Dare we hate or dislike those whom God loves? If we do,

can we really possess the Spirit of Christ? We really must face these elementary facts in our faith if prayer is to be anything more than a mere form. Our Lord not only says, *and pray for those who speak evil about you, and persecute you; that ye may be sons of your Father who is in the heavens* (Matt. 5:44-45).

We venture to think that large numbers of so-called Christians have never faced this question. To hear how many Christian workers and prominent ones also speak of others with whom they disagree, one must charitably suppose they have never heard that command of our Lord.

Hot-tempered people can only make frigid prayers.

Our daily life in the world is the best indication of our power in prayer. God deals with my prayers, not according to the spirit and tone, which I exhibit when I am praying in public or private, but according to the spirit I show in my daily life.

Hot-tempered people can only make frigid prayers. If we do not obey our Lord's command and love one another, our prayers are almost worthless. If we harbor an unforgiving spirit, it is almost wasted time to pray. Yet a prominent dean of one of our cathedrals was recently reported to have said that there are some people we can never forgive. If so, we trust that he uses an abridged form of the Lord's Prayer. Christ taught us to say *Forgive us … as we forgive.* And He goes further than this. He declares, *but if ye do not set men free from their trespasses, neither will your Father set you free from your trespasses* (Matt. 6:15). May we ever exhibit the Spirit of Christ and not forfeit our own much-needed forgiveness. How many of our readers who have not the slightest intention of forgiving their enemies, or even their offending friends, repeated the Lord's Prayer today?

Many Christians have never given prayer a fair chance. It is not through conscious insincerity, but from want of thought. The blame for it really rests upon those of us who preach and teach. We are prone to teach doctrines rather than doings. Most men desire to do what is right, but they regard the big things rather than the little failings in the life of love.

Our Lord goes so far as to say that even our gifts are not to be presented to God if we remember that our brother *has something against* us (Matt. 5:23). If He will not accept our gifts, is it likely He will answer our prayers? It was when Job ceased contending with his enemies (whom the Bible calls his friends) that the Lord *turned the captivity* and gave him twice as much as he had before (Job 42:10).

How slow we are, how unwilling we are, to see that our lives hinder our prayers. And how unwilling we are to act on love lines. Yes, we desire to "win" people. Our Lord shows us one way. Don't publish abroad his wrongdoings. Speak to him alone, and *thou hast gained thy brother* (Matt. 18:15). Most of us have rather pained our brothers.

Even the home life may hinder the prayer life. See what Peter says about how we should so live in the home that our *prayers not be hindered* (1 Peter 3:1-10). We would venture to urge every reader to ask God to search his heart once again and to show him if there is *any root of bitterness* towards anyone. We all desire to do what is pleasing to God. It would be an immense gain to our spiritual life if we would resolve not to attempt to pray until we had done all in our power to make peace and harmony between ourselves and any with whom we have quarreled. Until we do this, as far as lies in our power, our prayers are just wasted breath. Unkind feelings towards another hinder God from helping us in the way He desires.

A loving life is an essential condition of believing prayer. God challenges us again, today, to become fit persons to receive His abundant blessings. Many of us have to decide whether we will choose a bitter, unforgiving spirit, or the tender mercies and lovingkindness of our Lord Jesus Christ. Is it not amazing that anyone can halt between two opinions with such a choice in the balance? For bitterness harms the bitter more than anyone else.

And when ye are praying, forgive if ye have anything against anyone, so that your Father who is in the heavens will also forgive you (Mark 11:25). So said the blessed Master. Must we not then either forgive or cease trying to pray? What shall it profit a man if he gain all his time to pretend to pray, if he harbors unlove in his heart, which prevents real prayer? How the Devil laughs at us because we do not see this truth.

We have God's word for it that eloquence, knowledge, faith, liberality, and even martyrdom profit a man nothing – get hold of it [this idea] – nothing, unless his heart is filled with love (1 Cor. 13). "Therefore give us love."

(4) Refusal to do our part may hinder God answering our prayers. Love calls forth compassion and service at the sight of sin and suffering, both here and overseas. Paul's heart was *stirred*, "provoked" within him as he beheld the city full of idols (Acts 17:16). We cannot be sincere when we pray *Thy kingdom come* unless we are doing what we

can to hasten the coming of that kingdom by our gifts, our prayers, and our service.

We cannot be quite sincere in praying for the conversion of the ungodly unless we are willing to speak a word, or write a letter, or make some attempt to bring them under the influence of the gospel. Before one of Moody's great missions, he was present at a meeting for prayer, asking for God's blessing. Several wealthy men were there. One began to pray that God would send sufficient funds to defray the expenses. Moody at once stopped him. "We need not trouble God about that," he said quietly. "We are able to answer that prayer."

Praise is as important as prayer.

(5) Praying only in secret may be a hindrance. Children of a family should not always meet their father separately. It is remarkable how often our Lord refers to united prayer – agreed prayer. *When ye pray, say, Our Father* (Luke 11:2). *If two of you shall agree on earth as touching anything that they shall ask, it shall be done for them ... For where two or three are gathered together in my name, there am I in the midst of them* (Matt. 18:19-20).

We feel sure that the weakness in the spiritual life of many churches is to be traced to an inefficient prayer meeting or the absence of meetings for prayer. Daily morning prayers and evening prayers, even when reverent and without the unseemly haste, which is so often associated with them, cannot take the place of less-formal gatherings for prayer, in which everyone may take part. Can we not make the weekly prayer meeting a live thing and a living force?

(6) Praise is as important as prayer. We must enter into His gates with thanksgiving, and into His courts with

praise, and give thanks unto Him and bless His name (Psalm 100:4). At one time in his life, Praying Hyde was led to ask for four souls a day to be brought into the fold by his ministry. If on any day the number fell short of this, there would be such a weight on his heart that it was positively painful, and he could neither eat nor sleep. Then in prayer, he would ask the Lord to show him what was the obstacle in himself. He invariably found that it was the want of praise in his life. He would confess his sinfulness and pray for a spirit of praise. He said that as he praised God, seeking souls would come to him. We do not imply that we too should limit God to definite numbers or ways of working; but we do cry, "Rejoice! Praise God with heart and mind and soul."

It is not by accident that we are so often bidden to *rejoice in the Lord.* God does not want miserable children; and none of His children has cause for misery. The apostle Paul, the most persecuted of men, was a man of song. Hymns of praise came from his lips in prison and out of prison; day and night he praised his Savior. The very order of his exhortations is significant. *Always rejoice. Pray without ceasing. In every thing give thanks, for this is the will of God in Christ Jesus concerning you* (1 Thess. 5:16-18).

The will of God. Get that thought into your mind. It is not an optional thing.

Rejoice. Pray. Give thanks.

That is the order according to the will of God for you and for me. Nothing so pleases God as our praises, and nothing so blesses the man who prays as the praises he offers. *Delight thyself in the Lord; and he shall give thee the desires of thy heart* (Psalm 37:4).

A missionary who had received very bad news from home was utterly cast down. Prayer availed nothing to relieve the darkness of his soul. He went to see another missionary, no doubt seeking comfort. There on the wall was a motto card: "Try Thanksgiving." He did; and in a moment, every shadow was gone, never to return.

Do we praise Him enough to get our prayers answered? If we truly trust Him, we shall always praise Him.

> *For God nothing does nor suffers to be done*
>   *But thou would'st do thyself*
> *Could'st thou but see*
>   *The end of all events as well as He.*

One who once overheard Luther praying said, "Gracious God. What spirit and what faith is there in his expressions. He petitions God with as much reverence as if he were in the Divine presence, and yet with as firm a hope and confidence as he would address a father or a friend." That child of God seemed quite unconscious that *hindrances to prayer* existed.

After all that has been said, we see that everything can be summed up under one head. All hindrance to prayer arises from ignorance of the teaching of God's holy Word on the life of holiness He has planned for all His children, or from an unwillingness to consecrate ourselves fully to Him.

When we can truthfully say to our Father, "All that I am and have is thine," then He can say to us, "All that is mine is thine."

CHAPTER 12

WHO MAY PRAY?

I t is only two centuries ago that six undergraduates were expelled from the University of Oxford solely because they met together in each other's rooms for impromptu prayer. Whereupon George Whitfield wrote to the vice chancellor, "It is to be hoped that, as some have been expelled for extempore praying, we shall hear of some few others of a contrary stamp being expelled for extempore swearing." Today, thank God, no man in our land is hindered by his fellow men from praying. Any man may pray, but has every man a right to pray? Does God listen to anyone?

Who may pray? Is it the privilege – the right – of all men? Not everyone can claim the right to approach the king of our country. But there are certain persons and bodies of people who have the privilege of immediate access to our sovereign. The prime minister has that privilege. The ancient City of London Corporation can at any time lay its petition at the feet of the king. The ambassador of a foreign power may do the same. He has only to present himself at the gate of the palace of the king, and no power can stand between him and the monarch. He can go at once into the royal presence and present his request. But none of these has such ease of access and such loving welcome as the king's own son.

But there is the King of Kings, the God and Father of us all. Who may go to Him? Who may exercise this privilege, yes, this power, with God? We are told and there is much truth in the remark that in the most skeptical man or generation, prayer is always underneath the surface, waiting. Has it the right to come forth at any time? In some religions, it has to wait. Of all the millions in India living in the bondage of Hinduism, none may pray except the Brahmins. A millionaire merchant of any other caste must of necessity get a Brahmin, often a mere boy at school, to say his prayers for him.

Prayer is the result of the Holy Spirit dwelling within us.

The Muslim cannot pray unless he has learned a few phrases in Arabic; for his god only hears prayers offered in what they believe to be the holy language. Praise be to God, no such restrictions of caste or language stand between us and our God. Can any man, therefore, pray? Yes, you reply, anyone. But the Bible does not say so.

Only a child of God can truly pray to God. Only a son can enter His presence. It is gloriously true that anyone can cry to Him for help, for pardon and mercy. But that is scarcely prayer. Prayer is much more than that. Prayer is going into *the secret place of the most High* and abiding under the shadow of the Almighty (Psalm 91:1). Prayer is making known to God our wants and desires and holding out the hand of faith to take His gifts. Prayer is the result of the Holy Spirit dwelling within us. It is communion with God. Now, there can scarcely be communion between a king and a rebel. What communion hath light with darkness (2 Cor. 6:14)? In ourselves, we have no right to pray. We have access to God only through the Lord Jesus Christ (Eph. 2:12, 18).

Prayer is much more than the cry of a drowning man, of a man sinking in the whirlpool of sin: "Lord, save me. I am lost. I am undone. Redeem me. Save me." Anyone can do this, and that is a petition, which is never unanswered, and one, if sincere, to which the answer is never delayed. For "man cannot be God's outlaw if he would." But that is not prayer in the biblical sense. Even the lions, roaring after their prey, seek their meat from God; but that is not prayer.

We know that our Lord said, *for every one that asks receives* (Matt. 7:8). He did say so, but to whom?

He was speaking to His disciples (Matt. 5:1-2). Yes, prayer is communion with God, the "home life" of the soul, as one describes it. And I much question whether there can be any communion with Him unless the Holy Spirit dwells in the heart, and we have "received" the Son, and have the right to be called *sons of God* (John 1:12).

Prayer is the privilege of a child. Children of God alone can claim from the heavenly Father the things which He hath prepared for them that love Him. Our Lord told us that in prayer we should call God *our Father*. Surely only children can use that word. Paul says that it is *because ye are sons, God has sent forth the Spirit of his Son into your hearts, crying, Abba, Father* (Gal. 4:6). Is this what was in God's mind when, in dealing with Job's "comforters," He said, *My slave Job shall pray for you; for only because I will accept him* (Job 42:8)? It looked as if they would not have been *accepted* in the matter of prayer. But as soon as one becomes a "son of God," he must enter the school of prayer. *Behold, he prays*, said our Lord of a man as soon as he was converted (Acts 9:11). Yet that man had "said" prayers all his life. Converted men not only may pray, but must pray – each man for himself, and, of course, for others. But, unless and until we can truthfully call God "Father," we have no claim to be treated as children – as "sons," *heirs of God, and joint-heirs with Christ* – no claim at all. Do you say this is hard? Nay, surely it is natural. Has a child no privileges?

But do not misunderstand me. This does not shut any man out of the kingdom of heaven. Anyone, anywhere, can cry, "God be merciful to me, a sinner." Any man who is outside the fold of Christ, outside the family of God, however bad he may be, or however good he thinks he is, can this very moment become a child of God, even as he reads these words. One look to Christ in faith is sufficient: "Look and live." God did not even say "see" – He says just "look." Turn your face to God.

How did those Galatian Christians become *sons of God*? By faith in Christ. *For ye are all sons of God by faith in Christ Jesus* (Gal. 3:26). Christ will make any man a son of God by adoption and grace the moment he turns to Him in true repentance and faith. But we have no rightful claim even upon God's providence unless we are His child. We cannot say with any confidence or certainty, *I shall not want*, unless we can say, with confidence and certainty, *The Lord is my Shepherd*.

A child, however, has a right to his father's care, and love, and protection, and provision. Now, a child can only enter a family by being born into it. We become children of God by being *born again from above* and by being *born of water and of the Spirit* (John 3:3, 5), that is, by believing on the Lord Jesus Christ (John 3:16).

Having said all this as a warning, and perhaps as an explanation for why some people find prayer an utter failure, we hasten to add that God often hears and answers prayer even from those who have no legal right to pray, from those who are not His children, and may even deny that He exists. The Gospels tell us of not a few unbelievers who came to Christ for healing; and He never sent one away without the coveted blessing – never. They came as "beggars," not as "children." And even if "the children must first be fed," these others received the crumbs, yea, and more than crumbs that were freely given.

So today, God often hears the cry of unbelievers for temporal mercies. One case well known to me may be given as an illustration. My friend told me that he had been an atheist for many years. While an infidel, he had been singing for forty years in a church choir, because he was fond of music. His aged father became seriously ill two or three years ago and lay in great pain. The doctors were helpless to relieve the sufferer. In his distress for his father, the infidel choirman fell on his knees and cried, "O God, if there is a God, show Thy power by taking away my father's pain." God heard the man's piteous cry and removed the pain immediately. The atheist praised God and hurried off to his vicar to find out the way of salvation. Today he is out and out for Christ, giving his whole time to work for his newly found Savior. Yes, God is greater than His promises and is more willing to hear than we are to pray.

Perhaps the most striking of all prayers from the lips of unbelievers is that recorded of Caroline Fry, the author of

Christ Our Example. Although possessed of beauty, wealth, position, and friends, she found that none of them satisfied, and at length, in her utter misery, she sought God. Yet her first utterance to Him was an expression of open rebellion to and hatred of Him. Listen to it. It is not the prayer of a child:

"O God, if Thou art a God, I do not love Thee; I do not want Thee; I do not believe there is any happiness in Thee; but I am miserable as I am. Give me what I do not seek; give me what I do not want. If Thou canst, make me happy. I am miserable as I am. I am tired of this world; if there is anything better, give it me."

What a prayer! Yet God heard and answered. He forgave the wanderer and made her radiantly happy and gloriously fruitful in His service.

> *In even savage bosoms*
> *There are longings, strivings, yearnings*
> *For the good they comprehend not,*
> *And their feeble hands and helpless,*
> *Groping blindly in the darkness,*
> *Touch God's right hand in the darkness,*
> *And are lifted up and strengthened.*

Shall we, then, alter our question a little, and ask who has a right to pray? Only children of God in whom the Holy Spirit dwells. But, even so, we must remember that no man can come unashamed and with confidence to his Father in heaven unless he is living as a son of God should live. We cannot expect a father to lavish his favors upon erring children. Only a faithful and sanctified son can pray with the Spirit and pray with the understanding also (1 Cor. 14:15).

But if we are sons of God, nothing but sin can hinder our prayers. We, His children, have the right of access to God at any time, in any place. And He understands any form of prayer. We may have a wonderful gift of speech pouring itself out in a torrent of thanksgiving, petition, and praise like Paul; or we may have the quiet, deep, lover-like communion of John. The brilliant scholar like John Wesley and the *Oh, that all the shut-ins would speak out.* humble cobbler like William Carey are alike welcome at the throne of grace. Influence at the court of heaven depends not upon birth, or brilliancy, or achievement, but upon humble and utter dependence upon the Son of the King.

Moody attributed his marvelous success to the prayers of an obscure and almost unknown invalid woman. And truly, the invalid saints of England could bring about a speedy revival by their prayers. Oh, that all the shut-ins would speak out.

Do we not make a mistake in supposing that some people have a "gift" of prayer? A brilliant Cambridge undergraduate asked me if the life of prayer was not a gift and one which very few possessed. He suggested that, just as not everyone was musical, so not everyone is expected to be prayerful. George Müller was exceptional not because he had a gift of prayer, but because he prayed. Those who cannot "speak well," as God declared Aaron could, may labor in secret by intercession with those that speak the word. We must have great faith if we are to have great power with God in prayer, although God is very gracious and oftentimes goes beyond our faith.

or trembling hand dare put in motion any mighty force. Can I, dare I, move the Hand that moves the universe? No. Unless the Holy Spirit has control of me.

Yes, we need divine help for prayer and we have it. How the whole Trinity delights in prayer. God the Father listens: the Holy Spirit dictates: the eternal Son presents the petition and Himself intercedes; and so the answer comes down.

Believe me, prayer is our highest privilege, our gravest responsibility, and the greatest power God has put into our hands. Prayer, real prayer, is the noblest, the sublimest, the most stupendous act that any creature of God can perform.

It is, as Coleridge declared, "the very highest energy of which the human heart was capable." To pray with all your heart and strength – that is the last, the greatest achievement of the Christian's warfare on earth.

Lord, teach us to pray.

About the Author

Albert Ernest Richardson (1868) was educated at Oxford High School, London City Technical College and the University of Oxford obtaining a B.A in 1894, M.A. in 1897 and B.D. in 1901.

He initially offered his services as a missionary to the CMS in 1895 but this was deferred. He was ordained as a deacon in 1896 and as a priest in 1897 and between 1896 and 1898 was curate of St Clement's, Ipswich. In 1898 he was accepted as missionary and left for Lagos and then went overland to Tripoli as a member of the pioneer missionary party to Hausaland, Nigeria led by Bishop Herbert Tugwell. In 1902 again offered his services to the CMS and this time was accepted and in 1903 he went to Bombay. He authored *Hausaland and the Gospel* and is reputed to be the author of *The Kneeling Christian* which he wrote anonymously. His other works include *How to Live the Victorious Life* and *How to Know God: Meditations on the Secret of His Presence.*[12]

---

12   https://en.wikipedia.org/wiki/Albert_Richardson_(priest)

Pilgrim's Progress
Updated, Modern English. Includes Original Illustrations.

The best part of this book is the Bible verses added to the text. The original Pilgrim's Progress listed the Bible verse references, but the verses themselves are so impactful when tied to the scenes in this allegory, that they are now included within the twext of this book. The text is tweaked just enough to make it readable today, for the young and the old. Youngsters in particular will be drawn to the original illustrations included in this wonderful classic.

Available where books are sold